THE GOSPEL OF NEW LIFE

POPE
FRANCIS

THE GOSPEL OF
NEW LIFE

Following Christ, together,
on the path to holiness

Edited by
Giuliano Vigini

DARTON·LONGMAN+TODD

First published in English in 2015 by
Darton, Longman and Todd Ltd
1 Spencer Court
140 – 142 Wandsworth High Street
London SW18 4JJ

Published in Italian in 2015 by Edizione San Paolo
Piazza Soncino, 5, 20092 Cinisello Balsamo (Mi), Italy

ISBN: 978-0-232-53203-6

Phototypeset by Kerrypress Ltd, St Albans, Hertfordshire
Printed and bound by Imak Ofset, Turkey

Contents

Contents

Foreword by Vincent Nichols

The Gospel of New Life is a most welcome sequel to *The Church of Mercy*. Together they present Pope Francis's rich exposition of the unbreakable bond between God's mercy and the New Life which is his gift alone.

What is this New Life? Nothing less than God's life! God the Father of Mercy ceaselessly yearns that, by the outpouring of the Holy Spirit, we come to share fully in the risen life of Jesus, his beloved Son.

Moreover, all creation shall be imbued with this New Life. Creation is itself the fruit of God's mercy, freely loved into being from nothingness. Our sin disfigures God's work of art. Nevertheless, full of merciful love, God will definitively renew all that he has made; make it resplendent with his glory.

The Gospel of New Life inspires us, then, to look forward with unwavering hope to a 'new heaven' and a 'new earth', a final transformation 'where justice will abide, and whose blessedness will answer and surpass all the longings for peace which spring up in the human heart' (*Gaudium et Spes* 39).

Yet 'what lies ahead,' as the Holy Father insists, 'is the fulfilment of a transformation that in reality is already happening, beginning with the death and resurrection of Christ.' We are assured that 'Love has triumphed, mercy has been victorious. The mercy of God always triumphs!'

This inspiring truth at the heart of the Gospel of New Life emboldens us to respond to the call to conversion. Mercy and conversion are inseparable. Divine mercy opens up the space in which our lives may be turned right around. We come to see God's commandments as a merciful gift from God's hand. We come to welcome the Ten Commandments, Pope Francis explains, not as 'limitations of freedom' but 'signposts to freedom'. The heart of the Ten Commandments is, he writes, 'the love that comes from God and gives life meaning, love that makes us live not as slaves but as true sons and daughters. This is love that gives life to all relationships'. They 'are not a hymn to the 'no', they are to the 'yes'. A 'yes' to God, a 'yes' to love'.

Our 'yes' to God, our 'yes' to 'love', fills us with inexhaustible joy. This 'joy' is no 'transient tipsiness', the Holy Father tells us with a characteristically memorable turn of phrase. Rather it is a joy that endures because it is born from the moment Jesus looked at us and loved us, chose us to follow him. Of course, following Jesus, which includes saying 'yes' to the cross, is not always easy. Frequently we shout 'No!' Yet no matter our stubbornness of heart, no matter how low we fall, no matter how distant from God we feel, Jesus who died on the Cross, who descended into hell, has opened for us a way to a future of hope.

This same Jesus, risen and ascended into heaven, stays with us always, accompanying us to where he has already gone. With quiet gentleness Jesus convinces us that his Father, our Father, never grows tired of waiting for us, that he responds to our sinfulness with unfailing patience. This most patient Father breathes his life-giving Spirit into our dry old bones, clothing them with the glorious flesh of his incarnate Son. This is our holiness! No one is excluded from the invitation to journey along the path leading to it. It is a path, though, which I do not tread in isolation, under my own steam alone. No, we tread our pilgrim path together as members of the Church made holy by Jesus, and which is our Mother. From deep within the Church of Mercy, New Life comes to birth and is nurtured.

But the Church of Mercy does not keep New Life locked up. Securely enfolded within her embrace we are sent out. We go forth filled with the Holy Spirit to bring Jesus, the face of the Father's mercy, to those most distant and forgotten, to those most in desperate need of the joy that comes from meeting Jesus. However, we venture out to proclaim the Gospel of New Life with immense humility: we know well our dependence on divine mercy's tender caress – and that it may be experienced through those to whom we are sent!

We go out as missionaries of mercy announcing hope for the world to come. But this does not mean our sight is deflected from concern for this world and the present condition of those dwelling therein. Quite the opposite! The hope with which the Gospel of New Life fills our hearts impels us to be worthy stewards of creation's fruits. Our mission is to transform the 'throw away culture' of 'uncontrolled consumerism' into one which cherishes our God-given natural environment. This demands honouring the social dimension of that environment too. With irresistible passion Pope Francis denounces a world of abundance where hundreds of millions go hungry and an 'industry of destruction' that mercilessly discards as 'leftovers' the unemployed, the sick, the terminally ill, the old, and children, both born and unborn. Hope inspires us to cultivate an authentically human ecology that enables every person to enjoy a dignified life.

Pope Francis is adamant that the family is essential to the flourishing of this authentically human ecology. Against the culture of the temporary, he champions matrimony and the importance of raising children, who 'have a right to grow up in a family with a father and a mother capable of creating a suitable environment for the child's growth and emotional development'. The family, the 'first cell of society', is where we learn to share, learn to be merciful, learn to live the Gospel of New Life.

Please read attentively *The Gospel of New Life*. It will console you. It will challenge you too. To meet the challenge, Pope Francis directs us to the fairest flower of the Father's mercy, adorned in steadfast hope: Mary, Mother of Mercy and Mother of Hope. Mary, Mother of the Gospel of New Life. Strengthened by her maternal intercession:

'Let us accept the grace of Christ's resurrection. Let us be renewed by God's mercy, let us be loved by Jesus, let us enable the power of his love to transform our lives too; and let us become agents of this mercy, channels through which God can water the earth, protect all creation, and make justice and peace flourish'.

CARDINAL VINCENT NICHOLS
ARCHBISHOP OF WESTMINSTER

1

The Chains of the World

The desire for possession

One of the most reassuring truths is the Divine Providence. The prophet Isaiah presents it as the image of maternal love full of tenderness, and thus says: 'Can a woman forget her sucking child, that she should have no compassion on the son of her womb? Even these may forget, yet I will not forget you' (49:15). How beautiful is this! God does not forget us, not one of us! Everyone by name and surname. He loves us and doesn't forget. What a beautiful thought ... This invitation to trust in God finds a parallel on a page of Matthew's Gospel: 'Look at the birds of the air,' Jesus says, 'they neither sow nor reap nor gather into barns, and yet your heavenly Father feeds them ... Consider the lilies of the field, how they grow: they neither toil nor spin; yet I tell you, even Solomon in all his glory was not arrayed like one of these' (Matt. 6:26, 28–29).

However, thinking of the many people who live in precarious conditions, or even in a poverty offensive to their dignity, these words of Jesus could seem abstract, if not illusory. But actually they are relevant, now more than ever! They remind us that you cannot serve two masters: God and wealth. As long as everyone seeks to accumulate for themselves, there will never be justice. We must take heed of this! As long as everyone seeks to accumulate for themselves, there will be no justice. Instead, by entrusting ourselves to God's providence, and seeking his kingdom together, no one will lack the necessary means to live with dignity.

A heart troubled by the desire for possessions is a heart full of desire for possessions, but empty of God. That is why Jesus frequently warned the rich, because they greatly risk placing their security in the goods of this world, and security, the final security, is in God. In a heart possessed by wealth, there isn't much room for faith: everything is involved with wealth, there is no room for faith. If, however, one gives God his rightful place, that is first place, then his love leads one to share even one's wealth, to set it at the service of projects of solidarity and development, as so many examples demonstrate, even recent ones, in the history of the Church. And like this, God's Providence comes through our service to others, our sharing with others. If each of us accumulates not for ourselves alone but for the service of others, in this case, in this act of solidarity, the Providence of God is made visible. If, however, one accumulates only for oneself, what will happen when one is called by God? No one can take his riches with him, because – as you know – the shroud has no pockets! It is better to share, for we can take with us to heaven only what we have shared with others.

The road that Jesus points out can seem a little unrealistic with respect to the common mindset and to problems due to the economic crisis; but, if we think about it, this road leads us back to the right scale of values. He says: 'Is not life more than food, and the body more than clothing?' (Matt. 6:25). In order to ensure that no one lacks bread, water, clothing, a home, work, health, we need to recognise that all people are children of the Father who is in heaven and, therefore, brothers and sisters among us, and that we must act accordingly. I recalled this in the Message for Peace of 1 January this year: the way to peace is brotherhood and sisterhood – this going together, sharing things with one another.

In the light of the Word of God, let us invoke the Virgin Mary as Mother of Divine Providence. To her we entrust our lives, the journey of the Church and all humanity. In particular, let us invoke her intercession that we may all strive to live in a simple and sober manner, keeping in mind the needs of those who are most in need.

The false happiness of the transient

Joy is not transitory tipsiness: it is something quite different! True joy does not come from things or from possessing, no! It is born from the encounter, from the relationship with others, it is born from feeling accepted, understood and loved, and from accepting, from understanding and from loving; and this is not because of a passing fancy but because the other is a person. Joy is born from the gratuitousness of an encounter! It is hearing someone say, but not necessarily with words, 'You are important to me.' This is beautiful ... And it is these very words that God makes us understand. In calling you, God says to you, 'You are important to me, I love you, I am counting on you.' Jesus says this to each one of us! Joy is born from that! The joy of the moment in which Jesus looked at me.

Understanding and hearing this is the secret of our joy. Feeling loved by God, feeling that for him we are not numbers but people; and hearing him calling us. Becoming a priest or a religious is not primarily our own decision. I do not trust that seminarian or that woman novice who says, 'I have chosen this path.' I do not like this! It won't do! Rather, it is the response to a call and to a call of love. I hear something within me which moves me and I answer 'Yes'. It is in prayer that the Lord makes us understand this love, but it is also through so many signs that we can read in our life, in the many people he sets on our path. And the joy of the encounter with him and with his call does not lead to shutting oneself in, but to opening oneself; it leads to service in the Church.

St Thomas said, 'Bonum est diffusivum sui' – the Latin is not very difficult! – 'Good spreads.' And joy also spreads. Do not be afraid to show the joy of having answered the Lord's call, of having responded to his choice of love and of bearing witness to his gospel in service to the Church. And joy, true joy, is contagious; it is infectious ... it impels one forward. Instead when you meet a seminarian who is excessively serious, too sad, or a novice like this, you think, 'but something has gone wrong here'. The joy of the Lord is lacking, the joy that prompts you to serve, the joy of the encounter with Jesus which brings you to encounter others to proclaim Jesus. This is missing! There is no holiness in sadness, there isn't any!

St Teresa said, 'A saint who is sad is a sad saint.' It is not worth much ... When you see a seminarian, a priest, a sister or a novice with a long face, gloomy, who seems to have thrown a soaking wet blanket over their life, one of those heavy blankets ... which pulls one down ... Something has gone wrong! But please: never any sisters, never any priests with faces like 'chillies pickled in vinegar' – never! The joy that comes from Jesus. Think about this: when a priest – I say a priest, but also a seminarian – when a priest or a sister lacks joy he or she is sad; you might think, 'but this is a psychological problem'. No. It is true: that may be, that may be so, yes, it might. It might happen, some, poor things, fall sick ... It might be so. However, in general, it is not a psychological problem. Is it a problem of dissatisfaction? Well, yes!

But what is at the heart of this lack of joy? It is a matter of celibacy. I will explain to you. You seminarians, you sisters, you consecrate your love to Jesus, a great love. Your heart is set on Jesus and this leads us to make the vow of chastity, the vow of celibacy. However the vow of chastity and the vow of celibacy do not end at the moment the vow is taken, they endure ... It is a journey that matures, that develops towards pastoral fatherhood, towards pastoral motherhood, and when a priest is not a father to his community, when a sister is not a mother to all those with whom she works, he or she becomes sad. This is the problem. For this reason I say to you: the root of sadness in pastoral life is precisely in the absence of fatherhood or motherhood, an absence that comes from living this consecration unsatisfactorily – on the contrary it must lead us to fruitfulness. It is impossible to imagine a priest or a sister who is not fruitful: this is not Catholic! This is not Catholic! This is the beauty of consecration: it is joy, joy.

The sterile disease of pessimism

The joy of the gospel is such that it cannot be taken away from us by anyone or anything (cf. John 16:22). The evils of our world – and those of the Church – must not be excuses for diminishing our commitment and our fervour. Let us look upon them as challenges which can help us to grow. With the eyes of faith, we can see the light which the Holy Spirit always radiates in the midst of darkness, never forgetting that 'where sin increased, grace has abounded all the more' (Rom. 5:20). Our faith is challenged to discern how wine can come from water and how wheat can grow in the midst of weeds. Fifty years after the Second Vatican Council, we are distressed by the troubles of our age and far from naive optimism; yet the fact that we are more realistic must not mean that we are any less trusting in the Spirit or less generous.

One of the more serious temptations which stifles boldness and zeal is a defeatism which turns us into querulous and disillusioned pessimists, 'sourpusses'. Nobody can go off to battle unless he is fully convinced of victory beforehand. If we start without confidence, we have already lost half the battle and we bury our talents. While painfully aware of our own frailties, we have to march on without giving in, keeping in mind what the Lord said to Saint Paul: 'My grace is sufficient for you, for my power is made perfect in weakness' (2 Cor. 12:9). Christian triumph is always a cross, yet a cross which is at the same time a victorious banner borne with aggressive tenderness against the assaults of evil. The evil spirit of defeatism is brother to the temptation to separate, before its time, the wheat from the weeds; it is the fruit of an anxious and self-centred lack of trust.

In some places a spiritual 'desertification' has evidently come about, as the result of attempts by some societies to build without God or to eliminate their Christian roots. In those places 'the Christian world is becoming sterile, and it is depleting itself like an overexploited ground, which transforms into a desert' (John Henry Newman, letter of 26 January 1833, *The Letters and Diaries of John Henry Newman*, vol. III, Oxford, 1979, p. 204). In other countries, violent opposition to Christianity forces Christians to hide their faith in their own beloved homeland. This is another painful kind of desert. But family and the workplace can also be a parched place where faith nonetheless has to be preserved and communicated.

Yet 'it is starting from the experience of this desert, from this void, that we can again discover the joy of believing, its vital importance for us men and women. In the desert we rediscover the value of what is essential for living; thus in today's world there are innumerable signs, often expressed implicitly or negatively, of the thirst for God, for the ultimate meaning of life. And in the desert people of faith are needed who, by the example of their own lives, point out the way to the Promised Land and keep hope alive' (Benedict XVI, homily at the Holy Mass for the opening of the Year of Faith, 11 October 2012). In these situations we are called to be living sources of water from which others can drink. At times, this becomes a heavy cross, but it was from the cross, from his pierced side, that our Lord gave himself to us as a source of living water. Let us not allow ourselves to be robbed of hope!

The factory of destruction

When in the book of Revelation we hear the voice of the angel crying aloud to the four angels who were given power to damage the earth and the sea, 'Do not harm earth or sea or the trees' (Rev. 7:3), this brings to mind a phrase that is not here but in everyone's heart: 'Human beings are far more capable of doing this better than you.' We are capable of destroying the earth far better than the angels. And this is exactly what we are doing, this is what we do: destroy creation, destroy lives, destroy cultures, destroy values, destroy hope. How greatly we need the Lord's strength to seal us with his love and his power to stop this mad race of destruction! Destroying what he has given us, the most beautiful things that he has done for us so that we may carry them forward, nurture them to bear fruit. Created beings take control of everything, believing they are God, believing they themselves are in command. And wars, the wars that continue, they do not exactly help to sow the seed of life but to destroy. It is an industry of destruction. It is also a system, also of life, that when things cannot be fixed they are discarded: we discard children, we discard the old, we discard unemployed youth. This devastation has created the culture of waste. We discard people ... This is the first image that came to my mind as I listened to this reading. The second image comes from the same reading: 'A great multitude that no one could count, from every nation, from all tribes and peoples and languages' (7:9 NRSV) The nations, the tribes ... Now it's starting to get cold: those poor people, who have to flee for their lives, from their homes, from their people, from their villages, in the desert ... and they live in tents, they feel the cold, without medicine, hungry ... because the 'self-appointed god' has taken control of creation, of all that good that God has done for us. But who pays for this feast? They do! The young, the poor, those people who are discarded. And this is not ancient history: it is happening today. 'But Father, it is far away …' It is here too, everywhere. It is happening today. I will continue: it seems that these people, these children who are hungry, sick, do not seem to count, it's as if they were of a different species, as if they were not even human. And this multitude is before God and asks, 'Salvation, please! Peace, please! Bread, please! Work, please! Children and grandparents, please! Young people with the dignity of being able to work, please!' Among these are also those who are persecuted for their faith; 'Then one of the elders addressed me, saying, "Who are these, robed in white, and where have they come from?" … "These are they who have come out of the great ordeal; they have washed their robes and made them white in the blood of the Lamb"' (7:13–14 NRSV). And today, without exaggeration, […] I would like us to think of all these, the unknown saints. Sinners like us, worse off than us, destroyed, this multitude of people who are in great distress: most of the world is in tribulation. Most of the world is in tribulation. And the Lord sanctifies this people, sinners like us, but he sanctifies these people in tribulation.

Finally, there is a third image: God. First was the devastation; second was the victims; the third is God: 'Beloved, we are God's children now; it does not yet appear what shall be' (1 John 3:2), that is, hope. And this is the Lord's blessing that we still have: hope. Hope that he will have mercy on his people, pity on those who are in great tribulation and compassion for the destroyers so that they will convert. And so, the holiness of the Church goes on: with these people, with us, that we will see God as he is. What should our attitude be if we want to be part of this multitude journeying to the Father, in this world of devastation, in this world of war, in this world of tribulation? Our attitude [...] is the attitude of the Beatitudes. That path alone will lead us to the encounter with God. That path alone will save us from destruction, from destroying the earth, creation, morality, history, family, everything. That path alone. But it too will bring us through bad things! It will bring us problems, persecution. But that path alone will take us forward. And so, these people who are suffering so much today because of the selfishness of destroyers – of the destroyers of our brothers and sisters – these people struggle onwards with the Beatitudes, with the hope of finding God, of coming face to face with the Lord in the hope of becoming saints, at the moment of our final encounter with him.

May the Lord help us and give us the grace of this hope, but also the grace of courage to emerge from all this destruction, devastation, the relativism of life, the exclusion of others, exclusion of values, exclusion of all that the Lord has given us: the exclusion of peace. May he deliver us from this, and give us the grace to walk in the hope of finding ourselves one day face to face with him. And this hope, brothers and sisters, does not disappoint!

The paradox of abundance

The Church always seeks to be attentive and watchful regarding the spiritual and material welfare of people, especially those who are marginalised or excluded, in order to guarantee their safety and dignity.

The future of all nations is interconnected, more than ever before; they are like the members of one family who depend upon each other. However, we live in an era in which relations between nations are all too often damaged by mutual suspicion, which at times turns into forms of military and economic aggression, undermining friendship and rejecting or marginalising those who are already excluded. Those who lack their daily bread or decent employment are well aware of this. This is a picture of today's world, in which it is necessary to recognise the limits of approaches based on the sovereignty of each state, understood as absolute, and on national interests, frequently conditioned by small power groups.

Nowadays there is much talk of rights, frequently neglecting duties; perhaps we have paid too little heed to those who are hungry. It is also painful to see that the fight against hunger and malnutrition is hindered by 'market priorities', the 'primacy of profit', which have reduced foodstuffs to a commodity like any other, subject to speculation, also of a financial nature. And while we speak of new rights, the hungry are waiting, at the street corner, asking for the right to citizenship, asking for due consideration of their status, to receive a healthy, basic diet. They ask for dignity, not for alms.

These criteria cannot remain in the limbo of theory. Individuals and peoples ask that justice be put into practice: not only in the legal sense, but also in terms of contribution and distribution. Therefore, development plans and the work of international organisations must take into consideration the wish, so frequent among ordinary people, for respect for fundamental human rights in all circumstances and, in this case, the rights of the hungry person. When this is achieved, then humanitarian intervention, emergency relief and development operations – in their truest, fullest sense – will attain greater momentum and yield the desired results.

Interest in the production, availability and accessibility of foodstuffs, in climate change and in agricultural trade should certainly inspire rules and technical measures, but the first concern must be the individual person, who lacks daily nourishment, who has given up thinking about life, family and social relationships, and instead fights only for survival. At the inauguration of the First Conference on Nutrition

[...] in 1992, St Pope John Paul II warned the international community of the risk of the 'paradox of abundance', in which there is food for everyone, but not everyone can eat, while waste, excessive consumption and the use of food for other purposes is visible before our very eyes. This is the paradox! Unfortunately, this 'paradox' persists. There are few subjects about which there are as many fallacies as there are about hunger; few topics are as likely to be manipulated by data, statistics, by national security demands, corruption, or by grim references to the economic crisis. This is the first challenge that must be overcome.

The second challenge that must be addressed is the lack of solidarity; subconsciously we suspect that this word should be removed from the dictionary. Our societies are characterised by growing individualism and division; this ends up depriving the weakest of a decent life, and provokes revolts against institutions. When there is a lack of solidarity in a country, the effects are felt by all. Indeed, solidarity is the attitude that enables people to reach out to others and establish mutual relations on this sense of fellowship that overcomes differences and limits, and inspires us to seek the common good together.

Human beings, as they become aware of being partly responsible for the plan of creation, become capable of mutual respect, instead of fighting among themselves, damaging and impoverishing the planet. States, too, understood as communities of individuals and peoples, are called to act concertedly, to be willing to help each other through the principles and norms offered by international law. An inexhaustible source of inspiration, natural law, is inscribed in the human heart, and speaks to everyone in understandable terms: love, justice, peace, elements that are inseparable from each other. Like people, states and international institutions are called to welcome and nurture these values in a spirit of dialogue and mutual listening. In this way, the aim of feeding the human family becomes feasible.

Every woman, man, child and elderly person everywhere should be able to count on these guarantees. It is the duty of every state that cares for the well-being of its citizens to subscribe to them unreservedly, and to take the necessary steps to ensure their implementation. This requires perseverance and support. The Catholic Church also offers her contribution in this field through constant attention to the life of the poor, of the needy in all parts of the world; along the same lines, the Holy See is actively involved in international organisations and through numerous documents and statements. In this way, it contributes to identifying and adopting the criteria to be met in order to develop an equitable international system. These are criteria that, on the ethical plane, are based on the pillars of truth, freedom, justice and solidarity; at the same time, in the legal field, these same criteria include: the relationship between the right to be fed, and the right to life and to a dignified existence; the right to be protected by law, which is not always close to the reality of those who suffer hunger; and the moral obligation to share the world's economic wealth.

If we believe in the principle of the unity of the human family, based on the common paternity of God the Creator, and on the solidarity of human beings, no form of political or economic pressure which exploits the availability of foodstuffs can be considered acceptable. Political and economic pressure: here I am thinking about our sister and mother Earth, our planet, and about whether we are free from political and economic pressure and able to protect her, to prevent her from self-destruction. We have two conferences ahead of us, in Peru and France, that challenge us to protect the planet. I remember a phrase that I heard from an elderly man many years ago: 'God always forgives offences and abuses; God always forgives. Men forgive at times; but the Earth never forgives!' Protect our Sister Earth, our Mother Earth, so that she does not react with destruction. But, above all, no system of discrimination, de facto or de jure, linked to the ability to access the market of foodstuffs, must be taken as a model for international actions that aim to eliminate hunger.

The functioning of extreme consumerism

I feel bound to stress the close bond between these two words, 'dignity' and 'transcendent'.

'Dignity' was a pivotal concept in the process of rebuilding that followed the Second World War. Our recent past has been marked by the concern to protect human dignity, in contrast to the manifold instances of violence and discrimination, which, even in Europe, took place in the course of the centuries. Recognition of the importance of human rights came about as the result of a lengthy process, entailing much suffering and sacrifice, which helped shape an awareness of the unique worth of each individual human person. This awareness was grounded not only in historical events, but above all in European thought, characterised as it is by an enriching encounter whose 'distant springs are many, coming from Greece and Rome, from Celtic, Germanic and Slavic sources, and from Christianity which profoundly shaped them', (John Paul II, Address to the plenary sitting of the Council of Europe, 8 October 1998), thus forging the very concept of the 'person'.

Today, the promotion of human rights is central to the commitment of the European Union to advance the dignity of the person, both within the Union and in its relations with other countries. This is an important and praiseworthy commitment, since there are still too many situations in which human beings are treated as objects whose conception, configuration and utility can be programmed, and who can then be discarded when no longer useful, due to weakness, illness or old age.

In the end, what kind of dignity is there without the possibility of freely expressing one's thought or professing one's religious faith? What dignity can there be without a clear juridical framework which limits the rule of force and enables the rule of law to prevail over the power of tyranny? What dignity can men and women ever enjoy if they are subjected to all types of discrimination? What dignity can a person ever hope to find when he or she lacks food and the bare essentials for survival and, worse yet, when they lack the work which confers dignity?

Promoting the dignity of the person means recognising that he or she possesses inalienable rights which no one may take away arbitrarily, much less for the sake of economic interests.

At the same time, however, care must be taken not to fall into certain errors which can arise from a misunderstanding of the concept of human rights and from its misuse. Today there is a tendency to claim ever broader individual rights – I am tempted to say individualistic; underlying this is a conception of the human person as detached from all social and anthropological contexts, as if the person were a 'monad' (μονάς), increasingly unconcerned with other surrounding 'monads'. The equally essential and complementary concept of duty no longer seems to be linked to such a concept of rights. As a result, the rights of the individual are upheld, without regard for the fact that each human being is part of a social context wherein his or her rights and duties are bound up with those of others and with the common good of society itself.

I believe, therefore, that it is vital to develop a culture of human rights which wisely links the individual, or better, the personal aspect, to that of the *common good*, of the '*all of us*' made up of individuals, families and intermediate groups who together constitute society. In fact, unless the rights of each individual are harmoniously ordered to the greater good, those rights will end up being considered limitless and consequently will become a source of conflicts and violence.

To speak of *transcendent human dignity* thus means appealing to human nature, to our innate capacity to distinguish good from evil, to that 'compass' deep within our hearts, which God has impressed upon all creation. Above all, it means regarding human beings not as absolutes, but as *beings in relation*. In my view, one of the most common diseases in Europe today is the *loneliness* typical of those who have no connection with others. This is especially true of the elderly, who are often abandoned to their fate, and also of the young who lack clear points of reference and opportunities for the future. It is also seen in the many poor who dwell in our cities and in the disorientation of immigrants who come here seeking a better future.

This loneliness has become more acute as a result of the economic crisis, whose effects continue to have tragic consequences for the life of society.

Together with this, we encounter certain rather selfish lifestyles, marked by an opulence which is no longer sustainable and frequently indifferent to the world around us, and especially to the poorest of the poor. To our dismay we see technical and economic questions dominating political debate, to the detriment of genuine concern for human beings. Men and women risk being reduced to mere cogs in a machine that treats them as items of consumption to be exploited, with the result that – as is so tragically apparent – whenever a human life no longer proves useful for that machine, it is discarded with few qualms, as in the case of the sick, the terminally ill, the elderly who are abandoned and uncared for, and children who are killed in the womb.

This is the great mistake made 'when technology is allowed to take over' (Benedict XVI, *Caritas in veritate*, 71); 'the result is a confusion between ends and means' (*ibidem*). It is the inevitable consequence of a *'throwaway culture'* and an *uncontrolled consumerism*. Upholding the dignity of the person means instead acknowledging the value of human life, which is freely given us and hence cannot be an object of trade or commerce. As members of this Parliament [the General Assembly of Episcopal Conference of Italy], you are called to a great mission which may at times seem an impossible one: to tend to the needs, the needs of individuals and peoples. To tend to those in need takes strength and tenderness, effort and generosity in the midst of a functionalistic and privatised mindset which inexorably leads to a 'throwaway culture'. To care for individuals and peoples in need means protecting memory and hope; it means taking responsibility for the present with its situations of utter marginalisation and anguish, and being capable of bestowing dignity upon it.

The temptations of the pastor

Temptations, which seek to obscure the primacy of God and of his Christ, are 'legion' in the life of a pastor: they range from apathy, which ends in mediocrity, to the search for a quiet life that avoids renunciation and sacrifice. A hurried pastoral ministry is a *temptation* likened to her stepsister, that is, the acedia that leads to intolerance, as though everything were a burden. The presumption of those who delude themselves into thinking that they can rely on their own strength, on the abundance of their resources and structures, on the organisational strategies one knows how to put in place is a *temptation*. It is a *temptation* to sit in sadness, for as it extinguishes all hope and creativity, it also leaves one dissatisfied and therefore unable to enter the lives of our people and to understand them in the light of Easter morning.

If we distance ourselves from Jesus Christ, if our encounter with him loses its freshness, we will experience first hand only the sterility of our words and initiatives. For pastoral plans are useful, but our trust is placed elsewhere: in the Spirit of the Lord, who – in the measure of our docility – continually opens up the horizons of mission.

To avoid running aground on the rocks, our spiritual life cannot be reduced to a few religious moments. In the succession of days and seasons, in the unfolding of times and events, we learn to see ourselves by looking to the One who does not pass away: *spirituality* is a return to the essential, to that good that no one can take from us, the one truly necessary thing. Even in times of aridity, when pastoral situations become difficult and we have the impression that we have been left alone, it is a *mantle of consolation* greater than any bitterness; it is a *metre of freedom* from the judgement of the so-called 'common sense'; it is a *fount of joy*, which enables us to receive everything from the hand of God and to contemplate his presence in everything and everyone.

Let us never tire, therefore, of seeking the Lord – *of letting ourselves be sought by him* – of tending over our relationship with him in silence and prayerful listening. Let us keep our gaze fixed on him, the centre of time and history; let us make room for his presence within us: he is the principle and foundation of mercy which envelops our weaknesses and transforms and renews everything; he is the most precious thing we are called to offer to our people, who otherwise are left at the mercy of an indifferent society, if not in despair. Everyone lives by him, even if we ignore him. The lofty standard of holiness passes through him, the Man of the Beatitudes – a gospel passage that returns daily in my meditation: if we mean to follow him, no other way is given to us. In travelling this way with him we discover that we are a people and come to recognise with wonder and gratitude that all is grace – even the struggles and contradictions of human life – if these are lived with a heart open to the Lord, with the patience of an artisan and with the heart of a repentant sinner.

Do not take over the vineyard

[...] The prophet Isaiah (5:1, 7) and the Gospel of Mark (21:33, 43) employ the image of the Lord's vineyard. The Lord's vineyard is his 'dream', the plan which he nurtures with all his love, like a farmer who cares for his vineyard. Vines are plants which need much care!

God's 'dream' is his people. He planted it and nurtured it with patient and faithful love, so that it can become a holy people, a people which brings forth abundant fruits of justice.

But in both the ancient prophecy and in Jesus' parable, God's dream is thwarted. Isaiah says that the vine which he so loved and nurtured has yielded 'wild grapes' (5:2, 4); God 'expected justice but saw bloodshed, righteousness, but only a cry of distress' (5:7). In the Gospel, it is the farmers themselves who ruin the Lord's plan: they fail to do their job but think only of their own interests.

In Jesus' parable, he is addressing the chief priests and the elders of the people, in other words the 'experts', the managers. To them in a particular way God entrusted his 'dream', his people, for them to nurture, tend and protect from the animals of the field. This is the job of leaders: to nurture the vineyard with freedom, creativity and hard work.

But Jesus tells us that those farmers took over the vineyard. Out of greed and pride they want to do with it as they will, and so they prevent God from realising his dream for the people he has chosen.

The temptation to greed is ever present. We encounter it also in the great prophecy of Ezekiel on the shepherds (cf. ch. 34), which St Augustine commented upon in one of his celebrated sermons [...]. Greed for money and power. And to satisfy this greed, evil pastors lay intolerable burdens on the shoulders of others, which they themselves do not lift a finger to move (cf. Matt. 23:4).

We too, in the Synod of Bishops, are called to work for the Lord's vineyard. Synod Assemblies are not meant to discuss beautiful and clever ideas, or to see who is more intelligent ... They are meant to better nurture and tend the Lord's vineyard, to help realise his dream, his loving plan for his people. In this case the Lord is asking us to care for the family, which has been from the beginning an integral part of his loving plan for humanity.

We are all sinners and can also be tempted to 'take over' the vineyard, because of that greed which is always present in us human beings. God's dream always clashes with the hypocrisy of some of his servants. We can 'thwart' God's dream if we fail to let ourselves be guided by the Holy Spirit. The Spirit gives us that wisdom which surpasses knowledge, and enables us to work generously with authentic freedom and humble creativity.

To do a good job of nurturing and tending the vineyard, our hearts and our minds must be kept in Jesus Christ by 'the peace of God which passes all understanding' (Phil. 4:7). In this way our thoughts and plans will correspond to God's dream: to form a holy people who are his own and produce the fruits of the kingdom of God (cf. Matt. 21:43).

2

Changing the Heart

We are creatures, we are not God

'Rend your hearts and not your garments' (Joel 2:13). With these penetrating words of the prophet Joel, the liturgy [...] introduces us to Lent, pointing to conversion of heart as the chief characteristic of this season of grace. The prophetic appeal challenges all of us without exception, and it reminds us that conversion is not to be reduced to outward forms or to vague intentions, but engages and transforms one's entire existence beginning from the centre of the person, from the conscience. We are invited to embark upon a journey on which, by defying *routine*, we strive to open our eyes and ears, but especially to open our hearts, in order to go beyond our own 'backyard'.

Opening oneself to God and to one another. We know that this increasingly artificial world would have us live in a culture of 'doing', of the 'useful', where we exclude God from our horizon without realising it. But we also exclude the horizon itself!

Lent beckons us to 'rouse ourselves', to remind ourselves that we are creatures, simply put, that we are not God. In the little daily scene, as I look at some of the power struggles to occupy spaces, I think: these people are playing God the Creator. They still have not realised that they are not God.

And we also risk closing ourselves off to others and forgetting them. But only when the difficulties and suffering of others confront and question us may we begin our journey of conversion towards Easter. It is an itinerary which involves the cross and self-denial. Today's Gospel indicates the elements of this spiritual journey: prayer, fasting and almsgiving (cf. Matt. 6:1–6, 16–18). All three exclude the need for appearances: what counts is not appearances; the value of life does not depend on the approval of others or on success, but on what we have inside us.

The first element is prayer. Prayer is the strength of the Christian and of every person who believes. In the weakness and frailty of our lives, we can turn to God with the confidence of children and enter into communion with him. In the face of so many wounds that hurt us and could harden our hearts, we are called to dive into the sea of prayer, which is the sea of God's boundless love, to taste his tenderness. Lent is a time of prayer, of more intense prayer, more prolonged, more assiduous, more able to take on the needs of one another; a time of intercessory prayer, to intercede before God for the many situations of poverty and suffering.

The second key element of the Lenten journey is fasting. We must be careful not to practise a formal fast, or one which in truth 'satisfies' us because it makes us feel good about ourselves. Fasting makes sense if it questions our security, and if it also leads to some benefit for others, if it helps us to cultivate the style of the Good Samaritan, who bends down to his brother in need and takes care of him. Fasting involves choosing a sober lifestyle; a way of life that does not waste, a way of life that does not 'throw away'. Fasting helps us to attune our hearts to the essential and to sharing. It is a sign of awareness and responsibility in the face of injustice, abuse, especially to the poor and the little ones, and it is a sign of the trust we place in God and in his providence.

The third element is almsgiving: it points to giving freely, for in almsgiving one gives something to someone from whom one does not expect to receive anything in return. Gratuitousness should be one of the characteristics of the Christian, who aware of having received everything from God gratuitously, that is, without any merit of their own, learns to give to others freely. Today gratuitousness is often not part of daily life where everything is bought and sold. Everything is calculated and measured. Almsgiving helps us to experience giving freely, which leads to freedom from the obsession of possessing, from the fear of losing what we have, from the sadness of one who does not wish to share their wealth with others.

With its invitations to conversion, Lent comes providentially to awaken us, to rouse us from torpor, from the risk of moving forward by inertia. The exhortation which the Lord addresses to us through the prophet Joel is strong and clear: 'Return to me with all your heart' (Joel 2:12). Why must we return to God? Because something is not right in us, not right in society, in the Church, and we need to change, to give it a new direction. And this is called needing to convert! Once again Lent comes to make its prophetic appeal, to remind us that it is possible to create something new within ourselves and around us, simply because God is faithful, always faithful, for he cannot deny himself, he continues to be rich in goodness and mercy, and he is always ready to forgive and start afresh. With this filial confidence, let us set out on the journey!

Listening to the word of Jesus

The Gospel of Matthew, in chapter 17, presents the Transfiguration. Jesus 'took with him Peter and James and John his brother, and led them up a high mountain apart' (Matt. 17:1). The mountain in the Bible represents a place close to God and an intimate encounter with Him, a place of prayer where one stands in the presence of the Lord. There, up on the mount, Jesus is revealed to the three disciples as transfigured, luminescent and most beautiful. And then Moses and Elijah appear and converse with him. His face is so resplendent and his robes so white that Peter, awe-struck, wishes to stay there, as if to stop time. Suddenly from on high the voice of the Father resounds, proclaiming Jesus to be his most beloved Son, saying 'Listen to him' (17:5). This word is important! Our Father said this to these apostles, and says it to us as well: 'Listen to Jesus, because he is my beloved Son.' This week let us keep this word in our minds and in our hearts: 'Listen to Jesus!' And the Pope is not saying this, God the Father says it to everyone: to me, to you, to everyone, all people! It is like an aid for going forward on the path of Lent. 'Listen to Jesus!' Don't forget.

This invitation from the Father is very important. We, the disciples of Jesus, are called to be people who listen to his voice and take his words seriously. To listen to Jesus, we must be close to him, to follow him, like the crowd in the Gospel who chase him through the streets of Palestine. Jesus did not have a teaching post or a fixed pulpit, he was an itinerant teacher, who gave his teachings, teachings given to him by the Father, along the streets, covering distances that were not always predictable or easy. Follow Jesus in order to listen to him. But also let us listen to Jesus in his written word, in the Gospel. I pose a question to you: do you read a passage of the Gospel every day? [...] It is important! Do you read the Gospel? It is so good; it is a good thing to have a small book of the Gospel, a little one, and to carry in our pocket or in our purse and read a little passage in whatever moment presents itself during the day. In any given moment of the day I take the Gospel from my pocket and I read something, a short passage. Jesus is there and he speaks to us in the Gospel! Ponder this. It's not difficult, nor is it necessary to have all four books: we can have one of the Gospels, a small one, with us. Let the Gospel be with us always, because it is the word of Jesus, in order for us to be able to listen to him.

From the event of the Transfiguration I would like to take two significant elements that can be summed up in two words: *ascent* and *descent*. We all need to go apart, to ascend the mountain in a space of silence, to find ourselves and better perceive the voice of the Lord. This we do in prayer. But we cannot stay there! Encounter with God in prayer inspires us anew to 'descend the mountain' and return to the plain where we meet many brothers and sisters weighed down by fatigue, sickness, injustice, ignorance, poverty both material and spiritual. To these in difficulty, we are called to bear the fruit of that experience with God, by sharing the grace we have received. And this is curious. When we hear the word of Jesus, when we listen to the word of Jesus and carry it in our heart, this word grows. Do you know how it grows? By giving it to the other! The word of Christ grows in us when we proclaim it, when we give it to others! And this is what Christian life is. It is a mission for the whole Church, for all the baptised, for us all: listen to Jesus and offer him to others.

The courage of looking inside one's self

We all remember John's Gospel (4:1, 42) where Jesus meets the Samaritan woman in Sicar, near an old well where the woman went to draw water daily. That day, she found Jesus seated, 'wearied as he was with his journey' (John 4:6). He immediately says to her, 'Give me a drink' (4:7). In this way he overcomes the barriers of hostility that existed between Jews and Samaritans and breaks the mould of prejudice against women. This simple request from Jesus is the start of a frank dialogue, through which he enters with great delicacy into the interior world of a person to whom, according to social norms, he should not have spoken. But Jesus does! Jesus is not afraid. When Jesus sees a person he goes ahead, because he loves. He loves us all. He never hesitates before a person out of prejudice. Jesus sets her own situation before her, not by judging her but by making her feel worthy, acknowledged, and thus arousing in her the desire to go beyond the daily *routine*.

Jesus' thirst was not so much for water, but for the encounter with a parched soul. Jesus needed to encounter the Samaritan woman in order to open her heart: he asks for a drink so as to bring to light her own thirst. The woman is moved by this encounter: she asks Jesus several profound questions that we all carry within but often ignore. We, too, have many questions to ask, but we don't have the courage to ask Jesus! Lent, dear brothers and sisters, is the opportune time to look within ourselves, to understand our truest spiritual needs, and to ask the Lord's help in prayer. The example of the Samaritan woman invites us to exclaim, 'Jesus, give me a drink that will quench my thirst forever.'

The Gospel says that the disciples marvelled that their Master was speaking to this woman. But the Lord is greater than prejudice, which is why he was not afraid to address the Samaritan woman: mercy is greater than prejudice. We must learn this well! Mercy is greater than prejudice, and Jesus is so very merciful, very! The outcome of that encounter by the well was the woman's transformation: 'the woman left her water jar' (4:28), with which she had come to draw water, and ran to the city to tell people about her extraordinary experience. 'I found a man who told me all that I ever did. Can this be the Christ?' She was excited. She had gone to draw water from the well, but she found another kind of water, the living water of mercy from which gushes forth eternal life. She found the water she had always sought! She runs to the village, that village which had judged her, condemned her and rejected her, and she announces that she has met the Messiah: the one who has changed her life. Because every encounter with Jesus changes our lives, always. It is a step forward, a step closer to God. And thus every encounter with Jesus changes our life. It is always, always this way.

In this gospel passage we likewise find the impetus to 'leave behind our water jar', the symbol of everything that is seemingly important but loses all its value before the 'love of God'. We all have one, or more than one! I ask you, and myself: 'What is your interior water jar, the one that weighs you down, that distances you from God?' Let us set it aside a little, and with our hearts let us hear the voice of Jesus offering us another kind of water, another water that brings us close to the Lord. We are called to rediscover the importance and the sense of our Christian life, initiated in baptism, and, like the Samaritan woman, to witness to our brothers and sisters. A witness of what? Joy! To witness to the joy of the encounter with Jesus; for, as I said, every encounter with Jesus changes our life, and every encounter with Jesus also fills us with joy, the joy that comes from within. And the Lord is like this. So we must tell of the marvellous things the Lord can do in our hearts when we have the courage to set aside our own water jar.

The appeal to conversion

During the time of Lent, the Church, in the name of God, renews her appeal to repentance. It is the call to change one's life. Conversion is not the question of a moment or a time of the year, it is an undertaking that lasts one's entire lifetime. Who among us can presume not to be a sinner? No one. We are all sinners. The apostle John writes: 'If we say we have no sin, we deceive ourselves, and the truth is not in us. If we confess our sins, he is faithful and just, and will forgive our sins and cleanse us from all unrighteousness' (1 John 1:8–9). And that is what is happening during this celebration and throughout this day of penance. The Word of God that we heard introduces us to two essential elements of Christian life.

The first: *putting on the new nature*. The new self, 'created according to the likeness of God' (Eph. 4:24 NRSV), is born in baptism, when one receives the very life of God, which renders us his children and incorporates us into Christ and his Church. This new life permits us to look at reality with different eyes, without being distracted by things that don't matter and cannot last long, from things that perish with time. For this we are called to abandon the behaviour of sin and fix our gaze on what is essential. 'A man is more precious for what he is than for what he has' (*Gaudium et spes*, n. 35). This is the difference between life deformed by sin and life illumined by grace. From the heart of the person renewed in the likeness of God comes good behaviour: to speak always the truth and avoid all deceit; not to steal, but rather to share all you have with others, especially those in need; not to give in to anger, resentment and revenge, but to be meek, magnanimous and ready to forgive; not to gossip, which ruins the good name of people, but to look more at the good side of everyone. It is a matter of clothing oneself in the new self, with these new attitudes.

The second element: *abiding in love*. The love of Jesus Christ lasts for ever, it has no end because it is the very life of God. This love conquers sin and gives the strength to rise and begin again, for through forgiveness the heart is renewed and rejuvenated. We all know it: our Father never tires of loving and his eyes never grow weary of watching the road to his home to see if the son who left and was lost is returning. We can speak of God's hope: our Father expects us always, he doesn't just leave the door open to us, but he awaits us. He is engaged in the waiting for his children. And this Father also does not tire of loving the other son who, though staying at home with him the whole time, does not share in his mercy, in his compassion. God is not only at the origin of love, but in Jesus Christ he calls us to imitate his own way of loving: 'as I have loved you, that you also love one another' (John 13:34). To the extent to which Christians live this love, they become credible disciples of Christ to the world. Love cannot bear being locked up in itself. By its nature it is open, it spreads and bears fruit, it always kindles new love.

Where is my heart?

Holy Week begins with the festive procession with olive branches: the entire populace welcomes Jesus. The children and young people sing, praising Jesus.

But Holy Week continues in the mystery of Jesus' death and his resurrection. We have just listened to the Passion of our Lord. We might well ask ourselves just one question: Who am I? Who am I, before my Lord? Who am I, before Jesus who enters Jerusalem amid the enthusiasm of the crowd? Am I ready to express my joy, to praise him? Or do I stand back? Who am I, before the suffering Jesus?

We [hear] many, many names: the group of leaders, some priests, the Pharisees, the teachers of the law, who had decided to kill Jesus. They were waiting for the chance to arrest him. Am I like one of them?

We [hear] another name: Judas. Thirty pieces of silver. Am I like Judas? We have heard other names too: the disciples who understand nothing, who fell asleep while the Lord was suffering. Has my life fallen asleep? Or am I like the disciples, who did not realise what it was to betray Jesus? Or like that other disciple, who wanted to settle everything with a sword? Am I like them? Am I like Judas, who feigns love and then kisses the Master in order to hand him over, to betray him? Am I a traitor? Am I like those people in power who hastily summon a tribunal and seek false witnesses: am I like them? And when I do these things, if I do them, do I think that in this way I am saving the people?

Am I like Pilate? When I see that the situation is difficult, do I wash my hands and dodge my responsibility, allowing people to be condemned – or condemning them myself?

Am I like that crowd which was not sure whether they were at a religious meeting, a trial or a circus, and then chose Barabbas? For them it was all the same: it was more entertaining to humiliate Jesus.

Am I like the soldiers who strike the Lord, spit on him, insult him, who find entertainment in humiliating him?

Am I like the Cyrenean, who was returning from work, weary, yet was good enough to help the Lord carry his cross?

Am I like those who walked by the cross and mocked Jesus: 'He was so courageous! Let him come down from the cross and then we will believe in him!' Mocking Jesus …

Am I like those fearless women, and like the mother of Jesus, who were there, and who suffered in silence?

Am I like Joseph, the hidden disciple, who lovingly carries the body of Jesus to give it burial?

Am I like the two Marys, who remained at the tomb, weeping and praying?

Am I like those leaders who went the next day to Pilate and said, 'Look, this man said that he was going to rise again. We cannot let another fraud take place!', and who block life, who block the tomb, in order to maintain doctrine, lest life come forth?

Where is my heart? Which of these persons am I like? May this question remain with us throughout the entire Holy Week.

Opening up to the light

John's Gospel sets before us the story of the man born blind, to whom Jesus gives sight. The lengthy account opens with a blind man who begins to see, and it closes – and this is curious – with the alleged seers who remain blind in soul. The miracle is narrated by John in just two verses, because the evangelist does not want to draw attention to the miracle itself, but rather to what follows, to the discussions it arouses, also to the gossip. So many times a good work, a work of charity, arouses gossip and discussion, because there are some who do not want to see the truth. The evangelist John wants to draw attention to something that also occurs in our own day when a good work is performed. The blind man who is healed is first interrogated by the astonished crowd – they saw the miracle and they interrogated him – then by the doctors of the law who also interrogate his parents. In the end the blind man who was healed attains to faith, and this is the greatest grace that Jesus grants him: not only to see, but also to know him, to see in him, 'the light of the world' (John 9:5).

While the blind man gradually draws near to the light, the doctors of the law on the contrary sink deeper and deeper into their inner blindness. Locked in their presumption, they believe that they already have the light; therefore, they do not open themselves to the truth of Jesus. They do everything to deny the evidence. They cast doubt on the identity of the man who was healed, they then deny God's action in the healing, taking as an excuse that God does not work on the Sabbath; they even doubt that the man was born blind. Their closure to the light becomes aggressive and leads to the expulsion from the Temple of the man who was healed.

The blind man's journey, on the contrary, is a journey in stages that begins with the knowledge of Jesus' name. He does not know anything else about him; in fact, he says, 'The man called Jesus made clay and anointed my eyes' (9:11). Following the pressing questions of the lawyers, he first considers him a prophet (9:17) and then a man who is close to God (9:31). Once he has been banished from the Temple, expelled from society, Jesus finds him again and 'opens his eyes' for the second time, by revealing his own identity to him: 'I am the Messiah,' he tells him. At this point the man who had been blind exclaims, 'Lord, I believe!' (9:38), and he prostrates himself before Jesus. This is a passage of the Gospel that makes evident the drama of the inner blindness of so many people, also our own, for sometimes we have moments of inner blindness.

Our lives are sometimes similar to that of the blind man who opened himself to the light, who opened himself to God, who opened himself to his grace. Sometimes unfortunately they are similar to that of the doctors of the law: from the height of our pride we judge others, and even the Lord! Today, we are invited to open ourselves to the light of Christ in order to bear fruit in our lives, to eliminate unchristian behaviours; we are all Christians but we all, everyone, sometimes has unchristian behaviours, behaviours that are sins. We must repent of this, eliminate these behaviours in order to journey well along the way of holiness, which has its origin in baptism. We, too, have been 'enlightened' by Christ in baptism, so that, as St Paul reminds us, we may act as 'children of light' (Eph. 5:8), with humility, patience and mercy. These doctors of the law had neither humility nor patience, nor mercy!

I suggest that today […] you take the Gospel of John and read this passage from chapter 9. It will do you good, because you will thus see this road from blindness to light and the other evil road that leads to deeper blindness. Let us ask ourselves about the state of our own heart? Do I have an open heart or a closed heart? Is it opened or closed to God? Open or closed to my neighbour? We are always closed to some degree, which comes from original sin, from mistakes, from errors. We need not be afraid! Let us open ourselves to the light of the Lord. He awaits us always in order to enable us to see better, to give us more light, to forgive us. Let us not forget this! Let us entrust this Lenten journey to the Virgin Mary, so that we too, like the blind man who was healed, by the grace of Christ may 'come to the light', go forward towards the light and be reborn to new life.

The alphabet of the priestly spirit

The Lord continues to shepherd his flock through the ministry of bishops, assisted by priests and deacons. It is in them that Jesus makes himself present, in the power of his Spirit, and continues to serve the Church, nourishing within her faith, hope and the witness of love. These ministers are thus a great gift of the Lord for every Christian community and for the whole of the Church, as they are a living sign of the presence of his love.

Today we want to ask ourselves: what is asked of these ministers of the Church, in order that they may live out their service in a genuine and fruitful way?

In the 'Pastoral Letters' sent to his disciples, Timothy and Titus, the apostle Paul carefully pauses on the figures of bishop, priest and deacon, also on the figures of the faithful, the elderly and young people. He pauses on a description of each state of a Christian in the Church, delineating for bishops, priests and deacons what they are called to and what prerogatives must be acknowledged in those chosen and invested with these ministries. Today it is emblematic that, along with the gifts inherent in the faith and in spiritual life – which cannot be overlooked, for they are life itself – some exquisitely human qualities are listed: acceptance, temperance, patience, meekness, trustworthiness, goodness of heart. This is the alphabet, the basic grammar, of every ministry! It must be the basic grammar of every bishop, priest and deacon. Yes, this beautiful and genuine predisposition is necessary to meet, understand, dialogue with, appreciate and relate to brothers and sisters in a respectful and sincere way – without this predisposition it is not possible to offer truly joyous and credible service and testimony.

There is also a basic conduct which Paul recommends to his disciples and, as a result, to all those who are called to pastoral ministry, be they bishops, priests, presbyters or deacons. The apostle says that the gift which has been received must be continually rekindled (cf. 1 Tim. 4:14; 2 Tim. 1:6). This means that there must always be a profound awareness that one is not bishop, priest or deacon because he is more intelligent, worthier or better than other men; he is such only pursuant to a gift, a gift of love bestowed by God, through the power of his Spirit, for the good of his people. This awareness is very important and constitutes a grace to ask for every day! Indeed, a pastor who is cognisant that his ministry springs only from the heart of God can never assume an authoritarian attitude, as if everyone were at his feet and the community were his property, his personal kingdom.

The awareness that everything is a gift, everything is grace, also helps a pastor not to fall into the temptation of placing himself at the centre of attention and trusting only in himself. They are the temptations of vanity, pride, sufficiency, arrogance. There would be problems if a bishop, a priest or a deacon thought he knew everything, that he always had the right answer for everything and did not need anyone. On the contrary, awareness that he is the first recipient of the mercy and compassion of God, should lead a minister of the Church to always be humble and sympathetic with respect to others. Also, in the awareness of being called to bravely guard the faith entrusted (cf. 1 Tim. 6:20), he shall listen to the people. He is in fact cognisant of always having something to learn, even from those who may still be far from the faith and from the Church. With his confreres, then, all this must lead to taking on a new attitude marked by sharing, joint responsibility and communion.

Dear friends, we must always be grateful to the Lord, for in the person and in the ministry of bishops, priests and deacons, he continues to guide and shape his Church, making her grow along the path of holiness. At the same time, we must continue to pray that the pastors of our communities can be living images of the communion and of the love of God.

3

The Walk of a Christian Life

Lead the way

The terminology typical of scouting often uses the term 'way', as a meaningful value in the life of boys and girls, teenagers and adults. Therefore, I would like to encourage you to continue your journey which calls you to lead the way in the family; lead the way in creation; lead the way in the city. Walk and lead the way: walking, not wandering, and not quietly! Always walking, but leading the way.

Lead the way in the family. The family is always the cell of society, and is the primary place of education. It is the community of love and of life in which each person learns to relate to others and to the world; and thanks to the solid foundation acquired within the family a person is able to project him- or herself in society, to confidently enter other educational environments, such as the school, the parish, associations ... Thus, within this integration of the foundations assimilated in the family and 'outside' experiences, we learn to find our way in the world.

All vocations take their first steps within the family and bear the imprint throughout life. For a movement such as yours [adult Movement of Italian Catholic scouts] based on lifelong education and on educational choice, it is important to reaffirm that education in the family is a priority choice. For [...] Christian parents, the educational mission finds its specific source in the sacrament of matrimony, for which the task of raising children is a ministry of the utmost importance in the Church. Not only do parents have a certain educational obligation towards their children, but also children towards their siblings and towards their own parents, meaning that duty of reciprocal help in faith and in goodness. At times it happens that children are able, with their affection, with their simplicity, to reanimate the entire family. Dialogue between spouses, mutual discussion and listening are essential elements for a serene and fruitful family.

Lead the way in creation. Our time cannot ignore the issue of ecology, which is vital to human survival, nor reduce it to merely a political question: indeed, it has a moral dimension that affects everyone, such that no one can ignore it. As disciples of Christ, we have a further reason to join with all men and women of good will to protect and defend nature and the environment. Creation is, in fact, a gift entrusted to us from the hands of the Creator. All of nature that surrounds us is created like us, created together with us, and in a common destiny it tends to find its fulfilment and ultimate end in God himself – the Bible speaks of 'new heavens and a new earth' (cf. Isa. 65:17; 2 Pet. 3:13; Rev. 21:1). This doctrine of our faith is an even stronger stimulus for us to have a responsible and respectful relationship with Creation: in inanimate nature, in plants and in animals, we recognise the imprint of the Creator, and, in our fellow kind, his very image.

Living in closer contact with nature, as you do, entails not only respect for it but also the commitment to contribute concretely to eliminate the wastefulness of a society that increasingly tends to throw away goods which are still useful and which can be donated to the many who are in need.

Lead the way in cities. Living in neighbourhoods and cities, you are called to be as leaven which makes the dough rise, offering your sincere contribution to achieve the common good. It is important to know how to offer the gospel values with joy, in a fair and open discussion with various cultural and social bodies. In a complex and multicultural society, you are able to testify, with simplicity and humility to Jesus' love for each person, to try also new ways of spreading the gospel, faithful to Christ and faithful to your fellow human beings, who in the cities often experience wearing situations, and sometimes risk losing their way, losing the ability to see the horizon, failing to feel God's presence. Therefore, the true compass to offer these brothers and sisters is closeness of heart, a 'guided' heart, that is, with an awareness of God.

Dear brothers and sisters, may you continue to follow your path with hope in the future. [...] Let us recall St Paul (cf. 1 Cor. 9:24–27): he speaks of athletes who train with strict discipline to race for an ephemeral prize; the Christian, instead, trains to be a good missionary disciple of the Lord Jesus, listening assiduously to his word, always trusting in him, who never disappoints, pausing with him in prayer, seeking to be a living stone in the ecclesial community.

The power of prayers

In Luke's Gospel (18:1, 8) Jesus tells a parable about the need to pray always, never wearying. The main character is a widow whose insistent pleading with a dishonest judge succeeds in obtaining justice from him. Jesus concludes: if the widow succeeded in convincing that judge, do you think that God will not listen to us if we pray to him with insistence? Jesus' words are very strong: 'And will not God vindicate his elect, who cry to him day and night?' (Luke 18:7).

'Crying day and night' to God! This image of prayer is striking, but let us ask ourselves: Why does God want this? Doesn't he already know what we need? What does it mean to 'insist' with God?

This is a good question that makes us examine an important aspect of the faith: God invites us to pray insistently not because he is unaware of our needs or because he is not listening to us. On the contrary, he is always listening and he knows everything about us lovingly. On our daily journey, especially in times of difficulty, in the battle against the evil that is outside and within us, the Lord is not far away, he is by our side. We battle with him beside us, and our weapon is prayer which makes us feel his presence beside us, his mercy and also his help. But the battle against evil is a long and hard one; it requires patience and endurance, like Moses who had to keep his arms outstretched for the people to prevail (cf. Exod. 17:8–13). This is how it is: there is a battle to be waged each day, but God is our ally, faith in him is our strength and prayer is the expression of this faith. Therefore Jesus assures us of the victory, but at the end he asks, 'When the Son of man comes, will he find faith on earth?' (Luke 18:8). If faith is snuffed out, prayer is snuffed out, and we walk in the dark. We become lost on the path of life.

Therefore, let us learn from the widow of the Gospel to pray always without growing weary. This widow was very good! She knew how to battle for her children! I think of the many women who fight for their families, who pray and never grow weary. Today let us all remember these women who by their attitude provide us with a true witness of faith and courage, and a model of prayer. Our thoughts go out to them! Pray always, but not in order to convince the Lord by dint of words! He knows our needs better than we do! Indeed persevering prayer is the expression of faith in a God who calls us to fight with him every day and at every moment in order to conquer evil with good.

To obey the commandments

The Ten Commandments are God's gift. The word 'commandment' is not in style; it reminds people today of something negative, of someone's desire to impose restrictions, to put obstacles in life's way. Unfortunately history, even recent history, is marked by forms of tyranny, ideologies, types of logic that have imposed and oppressed and have not sought the good of people but, on the contrary, power, success and profit. The Ten Commandments come from a God who created us for love, from a God who made a covenant with humankind, a God who only wants our good. Let us give God our trust! Let us trust God! The Ten Commandments point out a path for us to follow, and they are a kind of 'ethical code' in order to build just societies attuned to humanity. How much inequality there is in the world! What hunger for food and for truth! What moral and material poverty stem from the rejection of God and from replacing him with so many idols! Let us be guided by these Ten Words that enlighten and direct those who seek peace, justice and dignity.

The Ten Commandments point to a way of freedom which finds fullness in the law of the Spirit that is not written on stone tablets but on the heart (cf. 2 Cor. 3:3): it is here that the Ten Commandments are written! It is fundamental to remember when God gave the Ten Commandments to the people of Israel through Moses. At the Red Sea the people had experienced great liberation; they had felt tangibly the power and faithfulness of God, of the God who sets us free. Now on Mount Sinai God himself points out to his people, and to all of us, the way to stay free, a way that is engraved in the human heart as a universal moral law (cf. Exod. 20:1–17; Deut. 5:1–22).

We must not see the Ten Commandments as limitations of freedom – no, that is not what they are – but rather as signposts to freedom. They are not restrictions but indicators of freedom. They teach us to avoid the slavery to which we are condemned by so many idols that we ourselves build – we have experimented with them so often in history, and we are still experimenting with them today. They teach us to open ourselves to a broader dimension than that of the material, and to show people respect, overcoming the greed for power, for possessions, for money, in order to be honest and sincere in our relations, to protect the whole of creation and to nourish our planet with lofty, noble spiritual ideals. Following the Ten Commandments means being faithful to ourselves and to our most authentic nature, and walking towards the genuine freedom that Christ taught us in the Beatitudes (cf. Matt. 5:3–12, 17; Luke 6:20–23).

The Ten Commandments are a law of love. Moses climbed the mountain to receive the tablets of the law from God. Jesus journeys in the opposite direction: the Son of God humbles himself, he comes down into our humanity to show us the profound meaning of these Ten Words: you shall love the Lord your God with all your heart, with all your soul and with all your strength and your neighbour as yourself (cf. Luke 10:27). This is the most profound sense of the Ten Commandments: the commandment of Jesus who bears within him all the commandments, the commandment of love. For this reason I say that the Ten Commandments are Commandments of Love. Here lies the heart of the Ten Commandments: the love that comes from God and gives life meaning, love that makes us live not as slaves but as true sons and daughters. This is love that gives life to all relationships: with God, with ourselves – we often forget this – and with others. True freedom is not that of following our own selfishness, our blind passions; rather it is that of loving, of choosing what is good in every situation. The Ten Commandments are not a hymn to the 'no', they are to the 'yes'. A 'yes' to God, a 'yes' to love, and since I say 'yes' to love, I say 'no' to non-love, but the 'no' is a consequence of that 'yes' which comes from God and makes us love.

Let us rediscover and live out the Ten Words of God! Let us say 'yes' to these 'ten paths of love', perfected by Christ, in order to defend human beings and direct them to true freedom! May the Virgin Mary accompany us on this journey.

Trust God's patience

The Second Sunday of Easter is also known as 'Divine Mercy Sunday'. What a beautiful truth of faith this is for our lives: the *mercy of God*! God's love for us is so great, so deep; it is an unfailing love, one which always takes us by the hand and supports us, lifts us up and leads us on.

In John's Gospel (20:19, 31), the apostle Thomas personally experiences this mercy of God, which has a concrete face, the face of Jesus, the risen Jesus.

Thomas does not believe it when the other apostles tell him, 'We have seen the Lord.' It isn't enough for him that Jesus had foretold it, promised it: 'On the third day I will rise.' He wants to see, he wants to put his hand in the place of the nails and in Jesus' side. And how does Jesus react? With *patience*: Jesus does not abandon Thomas in his stubborn unbelief; he gives him a week's time, he does not close the door, he waits. And Thomas acknowledges his own poverty, his little faith. 'My Lord and my God!': with this simple yet faith-filled invocation, he responds to Jesus' patience. He lets himself be enveloped by divine mercy; he sees it before his eyes, in the wounds of Christ's hands and feet and in his open side, and he discovers trust: he is a new man, no longer an unbeliever, but a believer.

Let us also remember Peter: three times he denied Jesus, precisely when he should have been closest to him; and when he hits bottom he meets the gaze of Jesus who patiently, wordlessly, says to him, 'Peter, don't be afraid of your weakness, trust in me.' Peter understands, he feels the loving gaze of Jesus, and he weeps. How beautiful is this gaze of Jesus – how much tenderness is there! Brothers and sisters, let us never lose trust in the patience and mercy of God!

Let us think too of the two disciples on the way to Emmaus: their sad faces, their barren journey, their despair. But Jesus does not abandon them: he walks beside them, and not only that! Patiently he explains the Scriptures which spoke of him, and he stays to share a meal with them. This is God's way of doing things: he is not impatient like us, who often want everything all at once, even in our dealings with other people. God is patient with us because he loves us, and those who love are able to understand, to hope, to inspire confidence; they do not give up, they do not burn bridges, they are able to forgive. Let us remember this in our lives as Christians: God always waits for us, even when we have left him behind! He is never far from us and, if we return to him, he is ready to embrace us.

I am always struck when I reread the parable of the merciful Father; it impresses me because it always gives me great hope. Think of that younger son who was in the Father's house, who was loved. And yet he wants his part of the inheritance; he goes off, spends everything, hits rock bottom, where he could not be more distant from the Father. But when he is at his lowest, he misses the warmth of the Father's house and he goes back. And the Father? Had he forgotten the son? No, never. He is there, he sees the son from afar, he was waiting for him every hour of every day, the son was always in his father's heart, even though he had left him, even though he had squandered his whole inheritance, his freedom. The Father, with patience, love, hope and mercy, had never for a second stopped thinking about him, and as soon as he sees him still far off, he runs out to meet him and embraces him with tenderness, the tenderness of God, without a word of reproach: he has returned! And that is the joy of the Father. In that embrace for his son is all this joy: he has returned!

God is always waiting for us, he never grows tired. Jesus shows us this merciful patience of God so that we can regain confidence, hope – always! A great German theologian, Romano Guardini, said that God responds to our weakness by his patience, and this is the reason for our confidence, our hope (cf. *Glaubensbekenntnis*, Würzburg, 1949, p. 28). It is like a dialogue between our weakness and the patience of God; it is a dialogue that, if we enter it, will grant us hope.

I would like to emphasise one other thing: God's patience has to call forth in us *the courage to return to him*, however many mistakes and sins there may be in our life. Jesus tells Thomas to put his hand in the wounds of his hands and his feet, and in his side. We too can enter into the wounds of Jesus, we can actually touch him. This happens every time that we receive the sacraments with faith. St Bernard, in a fine homily, says: 'Through the wounds of Jesus I can suck honey from the rock and oil from the flinty rock (cf. Deut. 32:13), I can taste and see the goodness of the Lord' (*On the Song of Songs*, 61:4). It is there, in the wounds of Jesus, that we are truly secure; there we encounter the boundless love of his heart. Thomas understood this. St Bernard goes on to ask: But what can I count on? My own merits? No, 'My merit is God's mercy. I am by no means lacking merits as long as he is rich in mercy. If the mercies of the Lord are manifold, I too will abound in merits' (*ibid.*, 5).

This is important: the courage to trust in Jesus' mercy, to trust in his patience, to seek refuge always in the wounds of his love. St Bernard even states: 'So what if my conscience gnaws at me for my many sins? "Where sin has abounded, there grace has abounded all the more" (Rom. 5:20)' (*ibid.*). Maybe someone among us here is thinking: my sin is so great, I am as far from God as the younger son in the parable, my unbelief is like that of Thomas; I don't have the courage to go back, to believe that God can welcome me and that he is waiting for me, of all people. But God is indeed waiting for you; he asks of you only the courage to go to him. How many times in my pastoral ministry have I heard it said, 'Father, I have many sins', and I have always pleaded, 'Don't be afraid, go to him, he is waiting for you, he will take care of everything.' We hear many offers from the world around us; but let us take up God's offer instead: his is a caress of love. For God, we are not numbers, we are important, indeed we are the most important thing to him; even if we are sinners, we are what is closest to his heart.

Adam, after his sin, experiences shame, he feels naked, he senses the weight of what he has done; and yet God does not abandon him. If that moment of sin marks the beginning of his exile from God, there is already a promise of return, a possibility of return. God immediately asks, 'Adam, where are you?' He seeks him out. Jesus took on our nakedness, he took upon himself the shame of Adam, the nakedness of his sin, in order to wash away our sin: by his wounds we have been healed. Remember what St Paul says: 'What shall I boast of, if not my weakness, my poverty?' Precisely in feeling my sinfulness, in looking at my sins, I can see and encounter God's mercy, his love, and go to him to receive forgiveness.

In my own life, I have so often seen God's merciful countenance, his patience; I have also seen so many people find the courage to enter the wounds of Jesus by saying to him, 'Lord, I am here, accept my poverty, hide my sin in your wounds, wash it away with your blood.' And I have always seen that God did just this – he accepted them, consoled them, cleansed them, loved them.

Dear brothers and sisters, let us be enveloped by the mercy of God; let us trust in his patience, which always gives us more time. Let us find the courage to return to his house, to dwell in his loving wounds, allowing ourselves be loved by him and to encounter his mercy in the sacraments. We will feel his wonderful tenderness, we will feel his embrace, and we too will become more capable of mercy, patience, forgiveness and love.

The courage of creativity

Our thoughts turn with great affection and gratitude to Chiara Lubich, an extraordinary witness to this gift, whose fruitful life brought the fragrance of Jesus to so many human realities and to so many parts of the world. Faithful to the charism from which it was born and which nourishes it, the Focolare Movement today faces the same task expected of the entire Church: to offer, with creativity and responsibility, its unique contribution to this new season of evangelisation. Creativity is important, it is impossible to go forward without it. It is important! And in this context I would like to assign three words to you who belong to the Focolare Movement and to those who, in various ways, share its spirit and ideals: contemplate, go forth, teach.

First and foremost, contemplate. Today more than ever we need to contemplate God and the wonders of his love, to abide in him who, in Jesus, came to place his tent in our midst (cf. John 1:14). To contemplate also means to live in the company of brothers and sisters and to break the Bread of communion and of fellowship with them, to cross the threshold together (cf. John 10:9) which leads us to the bosom of the Father (cf. John 1:18), because contemplation which has no place for others is a deception (cf. Apostolic Exhortation, *Evangelii Gaudium*, n. 281). Otherwise, it is narcissism.

Inspired by God in response to the signs of the times, Chiara Lubich wrote, 'The great attraction of modern times: to penetrate to the highest contemplation while mingling with everyone, one person alongside others' (*Spiritual Writings* 1, 27). In order to fulfil this it is necessary to broaden one's interiority regarding the measure of Jesus and the gift of his Spirit, to make contemplation the indispensable basis for a supportive presence and for effective, truly free and pure action.

I encourage you to be faithful to this ideal of contemplation, to persevere in the search for union with God and in mutual love with brothers and sisters. Draw on the treasures of the word of God and the tradition of the Church, on this yearning for communion and the unity which the Holy Spirit has evoked for our time. And give the gift of this treasure to everyone!

The second phrase – very important as it expresses the movement of evangelization – is to go out. To go out as Jesus went out from the bosom of the

Father to proclaim the word of love to all, even to the gift of his whole self on the wood of the cross. We must learn from him, from Jesus, this 'drive to go forth and give, to go out from ourselves, to keep pressing forward in our sowing of the good seed' (Apostolic Exhortation, *Evangelii Gaudium*, n. 21), to generously communicate God's love to all, with respect and, as the gospel teaches us – 'You received without pay, give without pay' (Matt. 10:8) – this sense of giving freely. Because redemption was given to us freely, forgiveness of sins cannot be 'paid for'. It was Christ who 'paid for' it once and for all! We must carry out the gratuitousness of the redemption with our brothers and sisters. Give freely, without payment, what we have received. And gratuitousness goes along with creativity: the two go together.

In order to do this, we must become experts in that art which is called 'dialogue' and which is not learned cheaply. We cannot be content with half measures, we cannot hesitate, but, with God's help, we can aim high and broaden our gaze! And to do this we must go out with courage 'to him outside the camp, bearing abuse for him' (Heb. 13:13). He is there in the trials and in the moans of our brothers and sisters, in the hurts of society and in the questions of the culture of our time. It hurts the heart when, before a church, before a humanity with so many wounds, moral wounds, existential wounds, wounds of war, which we all hear of every day, we see Christians beginning to do philosophical, theological, spiritual 'byzantinism'; rather, what is needed is a spirituality of going out. Go out with this spirituality: do not remain securely locked inside. This is not good. This is 'byzantinism'! Today we have no right to byzantinistic reflection. We must go out! Because – I have said this many times – the Church seems like a field hospital. And when one goes to a field hospital, the first task is to heal the wounded, not to measure cholesterol ... this will come later ... Is this clear?

And lastly, the third phrase: to teach. St John Paul II, in the Apostolic Letter *Novo Millennio Ineunte*, invited all the Church to become 'the home and the school of communion' (n. 43), and you have taken this instruction seriously. It is important to form, as the gospel requires, new men and women, and to that end a human school according to the measure of Jesus' humanity is necessary. Indeed, he is the New Man to whom, at any time, young people can look, with whom they can fall in love, whose way they can follow in order to face the challenges which lie before them. Without an appropriate formation of the new generations, it is illusory to think that a serious and lasting plan in service of a new humanity can be brought about.

Chiara Lubich coined an expression which is especially relevant: today, she said, we must form 'world men', men and women with the soul, the heart, the mind of Jesus and therefore capable of recognising and interpreting the needs, the concerns and the hopes which are harboured in the hearts of all people.

With you we will make big things

I would like to offer three short and simple thoughts for your reflection. In the book of Revelation (21:1, 5) we read the beautiful vision of St John: new heavens and a new earth, and then the Holy City coming down from God. All is new, changed into good, beauty and truth; there are no more tears or mourning … This is the work of the Holy Spirit: he brings us the new things of God. He comes to us and makes all things new; he changes us. The Spirit changes us! And St John's vision reminds us that all of us are journeying towards the heavenly Jerusalem, the ultimate newness which awaits us and all reality, the happy day when we will see the Lord's face – that marvellous face, the most beautiful face of the Lord Jesus – and be with him for ever, in his love.

You see, the new things of God are not like the novelties of this world, all of which are temporary; they come and go, and we keep looking for more. The new things which God gives to our lives are lasting, not only in the future, when we will be with him, but today as well. God is even now making all things new; the Holy Spirit is truly transforming us, and through us he also wants to transform the world in which we live. Let us open the doors to the Spirit, let ourselves be guided by him, and allow God's constant help to make us new men and women, inspired by the love of God which the Holy Spirit bestows on us! How beautiful it would be if each of you, every evening, could say: Today at school, at home, at work, guided by God, I showed a sign of love towards one of my friends, my parents, an older person! How beautiful!

A second thought. In the Acts of the Apostles Paul and Barnabas say that 'we must undergo many trials if we are to enter the kingdom of God' (14:22). The journey of the Church, and our own personal journeys as Christians, are not always easy; they meet with difficulties and trials. To follow the Lord, to let his Spirit transform the shadowy parts of our lives, our ungodly ways of acting, and cleanse us of our sins, is to set out on a path with many obstacles, both in the world around us but also within us, in the heart. But difficulties and trials are part of the path that leads to God's glory, just as they were for Jesus, who was glorified on the cross; we will always encounter them in life! Do not be discouraged! We have the power of the Holy Spirit to overcome these trials!

And here I come to my last point. [...] Remain steadfast in the journey of faith, with firm hope in the Lord. This is the secret of our journey! He gives us the courage to swim against the tide. Pay attention, my young friends: to go against the current; this is good for the heart, but we need courage to swim against the tide. Jesus gives us this courage! There are no difficulties, trials or misunderstandings to fear, provided we remain united to God as branches to the vine, provided we do not lose our friendship with him, provided we make ever more room for him in our lives. This is especially so whenever we feel poor, weak and sinful, because God grants strength to our weakness, riches to our poverty, conversion and forgiveness to our sinfulness. The Lord is so rich in mercy: every time, if we go to him, he forgives us. Let us trust in God's work! With him we can do great things; he will give us the joy of being his disciples, his witnesses. Commit yourselves to great ideals, to the most important things. We Christians were not chosen by the Lord for little things; push onwards towards the highest principles. Stake your lives on noble ideals, my dear young people!

The new things of God, the trials of life, remaining steadfast in the Lord. Dear friends, let us open wide the door of our lives to the new things of God which the Holy Spirit gives us. May he transform us, confirm us in our trials, strengthen our union with the Lord, our steadfastness in him: this is a true joy!

Let us go forward on the path to holiness

One of the great gifts from the Second Vatican Council was that of recovering a vision of the Church founded on communion, and grasping anew the principle of authority and hierarchy in this perspective. This has helped us to better understand that all Christians, in so far as they have been baptised, are equal in dignity before the Lord and share in the same vocation, that is, to sainthood (cf. *Lumen Gentium*, nn. 39–42). Now let us ask ourselves: what does this universal vocation to being saints consist in? And how can we realise it?

First of all, we must bear clearly in mind that sanctity is not something we can procure for ourselves, that we can obtain by our own qualities and abilities. Sanctity is a gift, it is a gift granted to us by the Lord Jesus, when he takes us to himself and clothes us in himself, he makes us like him. In his Letter to the Ephesians, the Apostle Paul states that 'Christ loved the church and gave himself up for her, that he might sanctify her' (5:25–26). You see, sainthood truly is the most beautiful face of the Church, the most beautiful face: it is to rediscover oneself in communion with God, in the fullness of his life and of his love. Sanctity is understood, then, not as a prerogative of the few: sanctity is a gift offered to all, no one excluded, by which the distinctive character of every Christian is constituted.

All this makes us understand that, in order to be saints, there is no need to be bishops, priests or religious: no, we are all called to be saints! So many times we are tempted to think that sainthood is reserved only to those who have the opportunity to break away from daily affairs in order to dedicate themselves exclusively to prayer. But it is not so! Some think that sanctity is to close your eyes and to look like a holy icon. No! This is not sanctity! Sanctity is something greater, deeper, which God gives us. Indeed, it is precisely in living with love and offering one's own Christian witness in everyday affairs that we are called to become saints. And each in the conditions and the state of life in which he or she finds him- or herself. But you are consecrated. Are you consecrated? Be a saint by living out your offering and your ministry with joy. Are you married? Be a saint by loving and taking care of your husband or your wife, as Christ did for the Church. Are you an unmarried baptised person? Be a saint by carrying out your work with honesty and competence and by offering time in the service of your brothers and sisters. 'But, father, I work in a factory; I work as an accountant, only with numbers; you can't be a saint there ...' Yes, yes you can! There, where you work, you can become a saint. God gives you the grace to become holy. God communicates himself to you. Always, in every place, one can become a saint, that is, one can open oneself up to this grace, which works inside us and leads us to holiness. Are you a parent or a grandparent? Be a saint by passionately teaching your children or grandchildren to know and to follow Jesus. And it takes so much patience to do this: to be a good parent, a good grandfather, a good mother, a good grandmother; it takes so much patience, and with this patience comes holiness – by exercising patience. Are you a catechist, an educator or a volunteer? Be a saint by becoming a visible sign of God's love and of his presence alongside us. This is it: every state of life leads to holiness, always! In your home, on the street, at work, at church, in that moment and in your state of life, the path to sainthood has been opened. Don't be discouraged to pursue this path. It is God alone who gives us the grace. The Lord asks only this: that we be in communion with him and at the service of our brothers and sisters.

At this point, each one of us can make a little examination of conscience [...]: how have we responded up to now to the Lord's call to sanctity? Do I want to become a little better, a little more Christian? This is the path to holiness. When the Lord invites us to become saints, he doesn't call us to something heavy, sad ... quite the contrary! It's an invitation to share in his joy, to live and to offer with joy every moment of our life, by making it become at the same time a gift of love for the people around us.

If we understand this, everything changes and takes on new meaning, a beautiful meaning, a meaning that begins with little everyday things. For example, a woman goes to the market to buy groceries and finds a neighbour there, so they begin to talk and then they come to gossiping and this woman says, 'No, no, no I won't speak badly about anyone.' This is a step towards sainthood, it helps you become more holy. Then, at home, your son wants to talk a little about his ideas: 'Oh, I am so tired, I worked so hard today ...' But you sit down and listen to your son, who needs it! And you sit down, you listen to him patiently: this is a step towards sainthood. Then the day ends, we are all tired, but there are the prayers. We say our prayers: this too is a step towards holiness. Then comes Sunday and we go to Mass, we take communion, sometimes preceded by a beautiful confession which cleans us a little. This is a step towards sainthood. Then we think of Our Lady, so good, so beautiful, and we take up the rosary and we pray it. This is a step towards sainthood. Then I go out to the street, I see a poor person in need, I stop and address him, I give him something: it is a step towards sainthood. These are little things, but many little steps to sanctity. Every step towards sainthood makes us better people, free from selfishness and being closed within ourselves, and opens us to our brothers and sisters and to their needs.

Dear friends, in the First Letter of St Peter this is asked of us: 'As each has received a gift, employ it for one another, as good stewards of God's varied grace: whoever speaks, as one who utters oracles of God; whoever renders service, as one who renders it by the strength which God supplies; in order that in everything God may be glorified through Jesus Christ' (1 Pet. 4:10–11). This is the invitation to holiness! Let us accept it with joy, and let us support one another, for the path to sainthood is not taken alone, each one for oneself, but is travelled together, in that one body that is the Church, loved and made holy by the Lord Jesus Christ. Let us go forward with courage on this path to holiness.

4

On the Streets of Humanity

Members of a Mother Church

We have pointed out many times in previous catecheses that one does not become Christian by oneself, that is, through one's own effort, autonomously; neither are Christians made in a laboratory, but they are created and they grow in the faith within that great body which is the Church. In this sense the Church is truly mother, our Mother Church – it is beautiful to say it this way: our Mother Church – a mother who gives us life in Christ and who lets us live with all the other brothers and sisters in the communion of the Holy Spirit.

In her motherhood, the Church has the Virgin Mary as a model, the most beautiful and most lofty model that there could be. This was already evidenced in the first Christian communities, and the Second Vatican Council expressed it in a wonderful way (cf. Dogmatic Constitution, *Lumen Gentium*, nn. 63–64). The motherhood of Mary is surely unique, singular, and was brought about in the fullness of time, when the Virgin gave birth to the Son of God, conceived through the power of the Holy Spirit. However, the motherhood of the Church is established in precise continuity with that of Mary, as her continuation in history. The Church, in the fruitfulness of the Spirit, continues to generate new children in Christ, always listening to the Word of God and in docility to his plan of love. The Church is mother. The conception of Jesus in Mary's womb, in fact, is the prelude to the birth of every Christian in the womb of the Church. From the moment that Christ is the firstborn among many brethren (cf. Rom. 8:29) and our first brother Jesus was born of Mary, he is the model, and we are all born of the Church. We understand, then, how the relationship which unites Mary and the Church is so deep: by looking at Mary we discover the most beautiful and most tender face of the Church; and by looking at the Church we recognise the sublime features of Mary. We Christians are not orphans, we have a mama, we have a mother, and this is great! We are not orphans! The Church is mother, Mary is mother.

The Church is our mother because she has given birth to us in baptism. Each time we baptise a baby, he or she becomes a child of the Church, who enters the Church. And from that day, like an attentive mama, she helps us grow in faith and shows us, with the strength of the Word of God, the path of salvation, defending us from harm. The Church has received from Jesus the precious treasure of the gospel, not to retain it for herself, but to give it generously to others, as a mama would do. In this service of evangelisation, the Church, committed as a mother, manifests her motherhood in a special way, to offer her children the spiritual nourishment which nurtures and makes the Christian life bear fruit. However, we are all called to receive with an open mind and heart the Word of God which the Church imparts every day, because this Word has the capacity to change us from within. Only the Word of God has this capacity to change us from the inside, from our deepest roots. The Word of God has this power. And who gives us the Word of God? Mother Church. She nurses us from childhood with this Word, she raises us throughout our life with this Word, and this is great! It is actually Mother Church who, with the Word of God, changes us from within. The Word of God which Mother Church gives us transforms us, makes our humanity pulse, not according to mundane flesh, but according to the Holy Spirit.

In her motherly solicitude, the Church strives to show the believers the path to follow in order to live a fruitful life of joy and peace. Illuminated by the light of the gospel and supported by the grace of the sacraments, especially the Eucharist, we can guide our decisions towards the good and withstand with hope and courage the times of darkness and the most tortuous paths. The path of salvation, through which the Church guides us and accompanies us with the strength of the gospel and the support of the sacraments, gives us the ability to defend ourselves against evil. The Church has the courage of a mother who knows she must defend her children against the dangers which arise from Satan's presence in the world, in order to lead them to the encounter with Jesus. A mother always protects her children. This defence also calls for vigilance: to be watchful for the snares and seduction of the Evil One. Because even though Satan was defeated by God, he always returns with his temptations; we know it, we are all tempted, we have been tempted and we are tempted. Satan comes 'like a roaring lion' (1 Pet. 5:8), the apostle Peter says, and it is up to us not to be naive, but to be vigilant and to resist, steadfast in the faith. To resist with the counsel of Mother Church, to resist with the help of Mother Church, who like a good mama always accompanies her children at difficult times.

This is the Church, this is the Church we all love, this is the Church I love: a mother who has the good of her children at heart and who is able to give her life for them. We must not forget, however, that the Church is not only the priests, or [...] bishops, no, she is all of us! The Church is all of us! Agreed? And we too are children, but also mothers of other

Christians. All who are baptised, men and women, together we are the Church. So often in our life we do not bear witness to this motherhood of the Church, to this maternal courage of the Church! So often we are cowards! Let us then entrust ourselves to Mary, that she as mother of our firstborn brother Jesus may teach us to have the same maternal spirit towards our brothers and sisters, with the sincere capacity to welcome, to forgive, to give strength and to instil trust and hope. This is what a mother does.

In the school of mercy

We have emphasised that the Church lets us grow and, with the light and strength of the Word of God, shows us the path of salvation, and defends us from evil. Today I would like to highlight a particular aspect of this educational work of our Mother Church, which is how *she teaches us works of mercy*.

A good educator focuses on the *essential*. She doesn't get lost in details, but passes on what really matters so the child or the student can find the meaning and the joy of life. It's the truth. In the gospel the essential thing is *mercy*. God sent his Son, God made himself human in order to save us, that is, in order to grant us his mercy. Jesus says this clearly, summarising his teaching for the disciples: 'Be merciful, even as your Father is merciful' (Luke

6:36). Can there be a Christian who isn't merciful? No. A Christian must necessarily be merciful, because this is the heart of the gospel. And faithful to this teaching, the Church can only repeat the same thing to her children: 'Be merciful', as the Father is, and as Jesus was. Mercy.

And thus the Church conducts herself like Jesus. She does not teach theoretical lessons on love, on mercy. She does not spread to the world a philosophy, a way of wisdom ... Of course, Christianity is also all of this, but as an effect, by reflex. Mother Church, like Jesus, teaches by example, and the words serve to illuminate the meaning of her actions.

Mother Church teaches us to give food and drink to those who are hungry and thirsty, to clothe those who are naked. And how does she do this? She does it through the example of so many saints, men and women, who did this in an exemplary fashion; but she does it also through the example of so many dads and mamas, who teach their children that what we have extra is for those who lack the basic necessities.

Mother Church teaches us to be close to those who are sick. So many saints served Jesus in this manner! And so many simple men and women, every day, practise this work of mercy in a hospital ward, or in a rest home, or in their own home, assisting a sick person.

Mother Church teaches us to be close to those who are in prison. 'But no, Father, this is dangerous, those are bad people.' But each of us is capable ... Listen carefully to this: each of us is capable of doing the same thing that that man or that woman in prison did. All of us have the capacity to sin and to do the same, to make mistakes in life. They are no worse than you and me! Mercy overcomes every wall, every barrier, and leads you always to seek the face of the man, of the person. And it is mercy which changes the heart and the life, which can regenerate a person and allow him or her to integrate into society in a new way.

Mother Church teaches us to be close to those who are neglected and die alone. That is what the blessed Teresa did on the streets of Calcutta; that is what has been and is done by many Christians who are not afraid to hold the hand of someone who is about to leave this world. And here, too, mercy gives peace to those who pass away and those who remain, allowing them to feel that God is greater than death, and that in abiding in him even the last parting is a 'see you again' ... The blessed Teresa understood this well! They told her, 'Mother, this is a waste of time!' She found people dying on the street, people whose bodies were being eaten by mice on the street, and she took them home so they could die clean, calm, touched gently, in peace. She gave them a 'see you again', to all of them ... And so many men and women like her have done this. And they are awaiting them, there [in heaven], at the gate, to open the gate of heaven to them. Help people die serenely, in peace.

This is how the Church is Mother, by teaching her children works of mercy. She learned this manner from Jesus, she learned that this is what's essential for salvation. It's not enough to love those who love us. Jesus says that pagans do this. It's not enough to do good to those who do good to us. To change the world for the better it is necessary to do good to those who are not able to return the favour, as the Father has done with us, by giving us Jesus. How much have we paid for our redemption? Nothing, totally free! Doing good without expecting anything in return. This is what the Father did with us and we must do the same. Do good and carry on!

How beautiful it is to live in the Church, in our Mother Church who teaches us these things which Jesus taught us. Let us thank the Lord, who has given us the grace of having the Church as Mother, she who teaches us the way of mercy, which is the way of life.

Offering our gifts to others

From the very beginning, the Lord has showered the Church with the gifts of his Spirit, thereby rendering her always vigorous and fruitful with the gifts of the Holy Spirit. Among these gifts, some can be identified as especially precious for the edification of, and for the journey of, the Christian community: these are called *charisms*. In this catechesis we want to ask ourselves: what exactly is a charism? How can we recognise it and embrace it? And most of all: should the fact that there is a diversity and a multiplicity of charisms in the Church be seen in a positive sense, as a good thing, or as a problem?

In common parlance, when a 'charism' is spoken of, it often means a talent, a natural ability. We says, 'This person has a special charism to teach. It is a talent he or she has.' Thus, it is often said, regarding an especially bright and engaging person, 'He or she is a charismatic person.' 'What does this mean?' 'I don't know, but he is charismatic.' And we say this. We don't know what we are saying, but we say, 'He is charismatic.'

In the Christian perspective, however, a charism is much more than a personal quality, a predisposition that one can be endowed with: a charism is *a grace, a gift bestowed by God the Father, through the action of the Holy Spirit*. And it is a gift which is given to someone not because he is better than others or because he deserves it: it is a gift that God gives him, because with his freely given love he can place him *in service to the entire community*, for the good of all. Speaking in a rather more human way, we say, 'God gives this quality, this charism to this person, not for himself, but in order that he may put it at the service of the whole community.'

An important thing that should be highlighted immediately is the fact that alone, *one cannot understand whether one has a charism*, and which one. Many times we have heard someone say: 'I have this quality, I can sing really well.' And no one has the courage to say, 'It's better to keep quiet, because you torture all of us when you sing!' No one can say, 'I have this charism.' It is within the community that the gifts the Father showers upon us bloom and flourish; and it is *in the bosom of the community* that one learns to recognise them as a sign of his love for all his children. So, each one of us should ask him- or herself: 'Is there a charism that the Lord has endowed me with, by the grace of his Spirit, and that my brothers and sisters in the Christian community have recognised and encouraged? And how do I act with regard to this gift: do I use it with generosity, placing it at the service of everyone, or do I overlook it and end up forgetting about it? Or perhaps it becomes a reason for pride in me, such that I always complain about others and insist on getting my way in the community?'

These are questions that we must ask ourselves: if there is a charism in me, if this charism is recognised by the Church, if I am happy with this charism or if I am a bit jealous of the charisms of others, whether I wanted or I want to have the charism. A charism is a gift: God alone bestows it!

The most beautiful experience, though, is the discovery of *all the different charisms* and all the gifts of his Spirit that the Father showers on his Church! This must not be seen as a reason for confusion, for discomfort: they are all gifts that God gives to the Christian community, in order that it may grow in harmony, in the faith and in his love, as one body, the Body of Christ. The same Spirit who bestows this diversity of charisms unites the Church. It is always the same Spirit. Before this multitude of charisms, our heart, therefore, must open itself to joy and we must think, 'What a beautiful thing! So many different gifts, because we are all God's children, all loved in a unique way.'

Never must these gifts become reasons for envy, or for division, or jealousy! As the apostle Paul recalls in chapter 12 of his First Letter to the Corinthians, all charisms are important in the eyes of God. At the same time, no one is irreplaceable. That is to say that within the Christian community, we need one another, and each gift received is fully realised when it is shared with one's brothers and sisters, for the good of all. This is the Church! And when the Church, in the variety of her charisms, is expressed in communion, she cannot be mistaken: it is the beauty and the power of the *sensus fidei*, of that supernatural sense of faith which is bestowed by the Holy Spirit in order that, together, we may all enter the heart of the gospel and learn to follow Jesus in our life.

Listening to the cry of the poor

This meeting of grassroots movements [participants in the World Meeting of Popular Movements] is a sign, it is a great sign, for you have brought a reality that is often silenced into the presence of God, the Church and all peoples. The poor not only suffer injustice, they also struggle against it!

You are not satisfied with empty promises, with alibis or excuses. Nor do you wait with arms crossed for NGOs to help, for welfare schemes or paternalistic solutions that never arrive; or if they do, then it is with a tendency to anaesthetise or to domesticate ... and this is rather perilous. One senses that the poor are no longer waiting. You want to be protagonists. You get organised, study, work, issue demands and, above all, practise that very special solidarity that exists among those who suffer, among the poor, and that our civilisation seems to have forgotten or would strongly prefer to forget.

Solidarity is a word that is not always well received. In certain circumstances it has become a dirty word, something one dares not say. However, it is a word that means much more than an occasional gesture of generosity. It means thinking and acting in terms of community. It means that the lives of all take priority over the appropriation of goods by a few. It also means fighting against the structural causes of poverty and inequality; of the lack of work, land and housing; and of the denial of social and labour rights. It means confronting the destructive effects of the empire of money: forced dislocation, painful emigration, human trafficking, drugs, war, violence and all those realities that many of you suffer and that we are all called upon to transform. Solidarity, understood in its deepest sense, is a way of making history, and this is what the popular movements are doing.

This meeting [...] is not shaped by an ideology. You do not work with abstract ideas; you work with realities such as those I just mentioned and many others that you have told me about. You have your feet in the mud, you are up to your elbows in flesh-and-blood reality. You carry the smell of your neighbourhood, your people, your struggle! We want your voices to be heard – voices that are rarely heard. No doubt this is because your voices cause embarrassment; no doubt it is because your cries are bothersome; no doubt because people are afraid of the change that you seek. However, without your presence, without truly going to the fringes, the good proposals and projects we often hear about at international conferences remain stuck in the realm of ideas and wishful thinking.

The scandal of poverty cannot be addressed by promoting strategies of containment that only tranquilise the poor and render them tame and inoffensive. How sad it is when we find, behind allegedly altruistic works, the other being reduced to passivity or being negated; or, worse still, we find hidden personal agendas or commercial interests. 'Hypocrites' is what Jesus would say to those responsible. How marvellous it is, by contrast, when we see peoples moving forward, especially their young and their poorest members. Then one feels a promising breeze that revives hope for a better world. May this breeze become a cyclone of hope. This is my wish.

This meeting of ours responds to a very concrete desire, something that any father and mother would want for their children – a desire for what should be within everyone's reach, namely *land*, *housing* and *work*. However, nowadays, it is sad to see that land, housing and work are ever more distant for the majority. It is strange but, if I talk about this, some say that the Pope is communist. They do not understand that love for the poor is at the centre of the gospel. Land, housing and work, what you struggle for, are sacred rights. To make this claim is nothing unusual; it is the social teaching of the Church. I am going to dwell on each of these briefly since you have chosen them as the core issues for this meeting.

Land. At the beginning of creation, God created man and woman, stewards of his work, mandating them to till and to keep it (cf. Gen. 2:15). I notice dozens of farmworkers (*campesinos*) here, and I want to congratulate you for caring for the land, for cultivating it and for doing so in community. The elimination of so many brother and sister *campesinos* worries me, and it is not because of wars or natural disasters that they are uprooted. Land- and water-grabbing, deforestation, unsuitable pesticides are some of the evils which uproot people from their native land. This wretched separation is not only physical but existential and spiritual as well, because there is a relationship with the land, such that rural communities and their special way of life are being put at flagrant risk of decline and even of extinction.

The other dimension of this already global process is hunger. When financial speculation manipulates the price of food, treating it as just another commodity, millions of people suffer and die from hunger. At the same time, tons of food are thrown away. This constitutes a genuine scandal. Hunger is criminal, food is an inalienable right. I know that some of you are calling for agrarian reform in order to solve some of these problems, and let me tell you that in some countries – and here I cite the *Compendium of the Social Doctrine of the Church* – 'agrarian reform is, besides a political necessity, a moral obligation'(*CSDC*, 300).

It is not just me saying this, it is in the *Compendium of the Social Doctrine of the Church*. Please carry on your struggle for the dignity of the rural family, for water, for life, and so that everyone can benefit from the fruits of the earth.

Second, *housing*. I said it and I repeat it: a home for every family. We must never forget that, because there was no room in the inn, Jesus was born in a stable; and that his family, persecuted by Herod, had to leave their home and flee into Egypt. Today there are so many homeless families, either because they have never had a home or because, for different reasons, they have lost it. Family and housing go hand in hand. Furthermore, for a house to be a home, it requires a community dimension, and this is the neighbourhood … and it is precisely in the neighbourhood where the great family of humanity begins to be built, starting from the most immediate instance, from living together with one's neighbours.

We live nowadays in immense cities that show off proudly, even arrogantly, how modern they are. But while they offer well-being and innumerable pleasures for a happy minority, housing is denied to thousands of our neighbours, our brothers and sisters including children, who are called elegant names such as 'street people' or 'without fixed abode' or 'urban camper'. Isn't it curious how euphemisms abound in the world of injustices! A person, a segregated person, a person set apart, a person who suffers misery or hunger: such a one is an 'urban camper'. It is an elegant expression, isn't it? You should be on the lookout – I might be wrong in some cases; but in general what lurks behind each euphemism is a crime.

We live in cities that throw up skyscrapers and shopping centres and strike big real estate deals … but they abandon a part of themselves to marginal settlements on the periphery. How painful it is to hear that poor settlements are marginalised or, worse still, earmarked for demolition! How cruel are the images of violent evictions, bulldozers knocking down the tiny dwellings, images just like those from a war. And this is what we see today.

You know that in the crowded slums where many of you live, values endure that have been forgotten in the rich centres. These settlements are blessed with a rich popular culture where public areas are not just transit corridors but an extension of the home, a place where bonds can be forged with neighbours. How lovely are cities that overcome unhealthy mistrust and integrate those who are different, even making such integration a new factor of development. How lovely are cities that, in their architectural design, are full of spaces that unite, connect and foster recognition of the other. So the line to follow is neither eradication nor marginalisation but urban integration. Moreover, not only must the word 'integration' replace all talk of eradication; it must also supplant those projects that aim to varnish poor neighbourhoods, prettify the outskirts and daub make-up on social ailments instead of curing them by promoting genuine and respectful integration. It is a sort of cosmetic architecture, isn't it? And it is the trend. So let us keep on working so that all families have housing and so that all neighbourhoods have adequate infrastructure (sewage, light, gas, asphalted roads); and I go on: schools, hospitals or first aid clinics, sports clubs and all those things that create bonds and unite, and, as I have already said, access to health care and education and to secure tenancy.

Third, *Work*. There is no worse material poverty – I really must stress this – there is no worse material poverty than the poverty which does not allow people to earn their bread, which deprives them of the dignity of work. But youth unemployment, casual or underground work, and the lack of labour rights are not inevitable. These are the result of an underlying social choice in favour of an economic system that puts profit above people. If economic profit takes precedence over the individual and over humanity, we find a throw-away culture at work that considers humanity in itself, human beings, as a consumer good, which can be used and then thrown away.

Today, a new dimension is being added to the phenomena of exploitation and oppression, a very harsh and graphic manifestation of social injustice: those who cannot be integrated, the excluded, are discarded, the 'leftovers'. This is the throw-away culture, and I would like to add something on this [...]. This happens when the deity of money is at the centre of an economic system rather than the human person. Yes, at the centre of every social or economic system must be the person, the image of God, created to 'have dominion over' the universe. The inversion of values happens when the person is displaced and money becomes the deity.

I remember a teaching from around the year 1200 that illustrates this point. A Jewish rabbi was explaining the story of the tower of Babel to his faithful. He recounted the extraordinary effort required to build it: the bricks had to be made, and to make the bricks one had to mix mud and fetch straw, knead the mud with the straw, then cut it into squares, then dry them, then fire them, and after the bricks were fired and then cooled, hoist them up to keep on building the tower.

If a brick fell – a brick was very costly, given all the work – if a brick fell, it was almost a national tragedy. Whoever dropped it was punished or suspended or whatever. But if a worker fell, nothing happened. That is the situation when the person is at the service of the deity money – so said a Jewish rabbi in the year 1200, explaining such terrible incidents.

And so, thinking about throw-away matter, we must also turn our attention to what is going on in our society. I am repeating what I have already said in *Evangelii Gaudium*. Today children are disposed of because the birth rate in many of the world's countries has fallen, or because there is no food, or because they are killed before being born – children are thrown away.

The elderly are discarded, well, because they are useless, they are not productive. Neither children nor the elderly produce, and so, with more or less sophisticated systems, they are slowly being abandoned. And in the current period of economic crisis, now that it is necessary to regain a certain equilibrium, we are witnessing a third very painful disposal – the disposal of young people [...]. Millions of young people are discarded from work, are unemployed.

In European countries where statistics are very clear, and specifically here in Italy, slightly more than 40 per cent of young people are unemployed. Do you know what 40 per cent of young people means? A whole generation is being cancelled, in order to restore the balance sheet. In another European country, it is over 50 per cent and up to 60 per cent in its southern region. These are clear counts of discarded debris. So in addition to discarding children and the elderly who do not produce, a generation of young people is to be sacrificed, people thrown away, in order to prop up and rebalance a system with the deity money at its centre and not the human person.

Despite this throw-away culture, this culture of leftovers, so many of you who are excluded workers, the discards of this system, have been inventing your own work with materials that seemed to be devoid of further productive value ... But with the craftsmanship God gave you, with your inventiveness, your solidarity, your community work, your popular economy, you have managed to succeed, you are succeeding ... And let me tell you, besides work, this is poetry. I thank you.

From now on every worker, within the formal system of salaried employment or outside it, should have the right to decent remuneration, to social security and to a pension. Among you here are waste-collectors, recyclers, peddlers, seamstresses or tailors, artisans, fishermen, farmworkers, builders, miners, workers in previously abandoned enterprises, members of all kinds of cooperatives and workers in grass-roots jobs who are excluded from labour rights, who are denied the possibility of unionising, whose income is neither adequate nor stable. Today I want to join my voice to yours and support you in your struggle.

During this meeting, you have also talked about *peace* and *ecology*. It is logical. There cannot be land, there cannot be housing, there cannot be work if we do not have peace and if we destroy the planet. These are such important topics that the peoples of the world and their popular organisations cannot fail to debate them. This cannot just remain in the hands of political leaders. All peoples of the earth, all men and women of good will – all of us must raise our voices in defence of these two precious gifts: peace and nature, or 'Sister Mother Earth' as St Francis of Assisi called her.

Recently I said and now I repeat, we are going through World War Three, but in instalments. There are economic systems that must make war in order to survive. Accordingly, arms are manufactured and sold and, with that, the balance sheets of economies that sacrifice human beings at the feet of the idol of money are clearly rendered healthy. And no thought is given to hungry children in refugee camps; no thought is given to the forcibly displaced; no thought is given to destroyed homes; no thought is given, finally, to so many destroyed lives. How much suffering, how much destruction, how much grief. Today, dear brothers and sisters, in all parts of the earth, in all nations, in every heart and in grass-roots movements, the cry wells up for peace: war no more!

An economic system centred on the deity money also needs to plunder nature to sustain consumption at the frenetic level it needs. Climate change, the loss of biodiversity, deforestation are already showing their devastating effects in terrible cataclysms, which we see and from which you the humble suffer most – you who live near the coast in precarious dwellings, or so economically vulnerable that you lose everything due to a natural disaster. Brothers and sisters, creation is not a possession that we can dispose of as we wish; much less is it the property of some, of only a few. Creation is a gift, it is a present, it is a marvellous gift given to us by God so that we might care for it and use it, always gratefully and always respectfully, for the benefit of everyone.

We talk about land, work, housing. We talk about working for peace and taking care of nature. Why are we accustomed to seeing decent work destroyed, countless families evicted, rural farmworkers driven off the land, war waged and nature abused? Because in this system humanity, the human person, has been removed from the centre and replaced by something else. Because idolatrous worship is devoted to money. Because indifference has been globalised: 'Why should I care what happens to others as long as I can defend what's mine?' *Because the world has forgotten God, who is Father;* and by setting God aside, it has made itself an orphan.

Some of you said that this system cannot endure. We must change it. We must put human dignity back at the centre and on that pillar build the alternative social structures we need. This must be done with courage but also with intelligence, with tenacity but without fanaticism, with passion yet without violence. And all of us together, addressing the conflicts without getting trapped in them, always seeking to resolve the tensions in order to reach a higher plane of unity, of peace and of justice. We Christians have something very lovely, a guide to action, a programme we could call revolutionary. I earnestly recommend that you read it: the Beatitudes in St Matthew chapter 5 (cf. Matt. 5:3) and in St Luke chapter 6 (cf. Luke 6:20); and the Last Judgment passage in St Matthew chapter 25. This is what I told the young people at Rio de Janeiro: with these passages, you have the plan of action.

I know that you are persons of different religions, trades, ideas, cultures, countries, continents. Here and now you are practising the culture of encounter, so different from the xenophobia, discrimination and intolerance which we witness so often. Among the excluded, one finds an encounter of cultures where the aggregate does not wipe out the particularities. That is why I like the image of the polyhedron, a geometric figure with many different facets. The polyhedron reflects the confluence of all the partialities that in it keep their originality. Nothing is dissolved, nothing is destroyed, nothing is dominated, everything is integrated. Nowadays you too are looking for that synthesis between the local and the global. I know that you work daily in what is close at hand and concrete, in your area, your neighbourhood, your work place. I also invite you to keep seeking that broader perspective so that our dreams might fly high and embrace the whole.

With all this I attach great importance to the proposal which some of you have shared with me, that these movements – these experiences of solidarity which grow up from below, from the subsoil of the planet – should come together, be more coordinated, keep on meeting one another as you have done these days. But be careful, it is never good to confine a movement in rigid structures, so I say you should keep on meeting. Even worse is the attempt to absorb movements, direct or dominate them – unfettered movements have their own dynamic; nevertheless, yes, we must try to walk together. Here we are in this Old Synod Hall (now there is a new one), and synod means precisely 'to walk together'. May this be a symbol of the process that you have begun and are carrying forward.

Grass-roots movements express the urgent need to revitalise our democracies, so often hijacked by innumerable factors. It is impossible to imagine a future for society without the active participation of great majorities as protagonists, and such proactive participation overflows the logical procedures of formal democracy. Moving towards a world of lasting peace and justice calls us to go beyond paternalistic forms of assistance; it calls us to create new forms of participation that include popular movements and invigorate local, national and international governing structures with that torrent of moral energy that springs from including the excluded in the building of a common destiny. And all this with a constructive spirit, without resentment, with love.

I accompany you wholeheartedly on this journey. From our hearts let us say together: no family without housing, no farmworker without land, no worker without rights, no one without the dignity that work provides.

The challenge of a family

As pastors close to your community and attentive to the needs of the people, you know well the complexity of the situation and the pressing challenges to which the mission of the Church is subjected, also in Europe. As I wrote in the Apostolic Exhortation *Evangelii Gaudium*, we are called to be a Church which 'goes forth', moving from the centre to the peripheries to go towards all, without fear and without diffidence, with apostolic courage (n. 20). How many brothers and sisters, how many situations, how many contexts, even the most difficult, are in need of the light of the gospel!

I would like to thank you, dear brothers, for the commitment with which you have welcomed this text. I know that this document is increasingly the object of deep pastoral reflection and the starting point for paths of faith and evangelisation in many parishes, communities and groups. This too is a sign of communion and the unity of the Church.

The theme of your plenary, 'Family and the Future of Europe', presents an important occasion to reflect together on how to value the family as a precious resource for pastoral renewal. I feel it is important for pastors and families to work together in a spirit of humility and sincere dialogue so that the respective parish communities may become a 'family of families'. In this context, interesting experiences have blossomed, which call for proper attention in view of furthering fruitful cooperation in your respective local churches: engaged couples who seriously live marriage preparation; married couples who welcome foster or adopted children; groups of families who in parishes or in movements help each other on the path of life and faith. There is no lack of experience of different types of pastoral care of the family and of political and social commitment in supporting families, both those who live traditional married lives and those marked by problems or by break-up. It is important to take these important experiences in the various contexts and in the life of the men and women of today, as a propitious time to exercise careful discernment in order to 'network' them, thus involving other diocesan communities.

The cooperation between pastors and families also extends to the field of education. Indeed, the family, which already fulfils its role with regard to its members, is a school of humanity, brotherhood and sisterhood, love, communion, which forms mature and responsible citizens. Open cooperation between the clergy and families will favour the maturation of a spirit of justice, of solidarity, of peace and the courage of one's convictions. This will come about by supporting parents in their responsibility to educate their children, thus protecting their inalienable right to provide their children with the education they deem most suitable. Parents, in fact, remain the first and foremost educators of their children, thus they have the right to educate them according to their moral and religious convictions. In this way, you will be able to outline common and coordinated pastoral directives necessary to promote and effectively support Catholic schools.

For the culture of marriage

I would like to begin by sharing a reflection on the theme of your colloquium [International Colloquium sponsored by the Congregation for the Doctrine of the Faith]. 'Complementarity' is a precious word, with multiple values. It can refer to various situations in which one component completes another or compensates for a lack in the other. However, complementarity is much more than this. Christians find its meaning in the First Letter of Paul to the Corinthians, where the apostle says that the Spirit has endowed each one with different gifts in order that, as limbs join the human body for the good of the organism as a whole, so the talents of each one contribute to the benefit of all (cf. 1 Cor. 12). To reflect upon complementarity is but to ponder the dynamic harmonies which lie at the heart of all creation. This is a key word: harmony. The Creator made every complementarity, so that the Holy Spirit, the Author of harmony, could create this harmony.

It is fitting that you have gathered here in this international colloquium to explore the theme of the complementarity between man and woman. In effect, this complementarity lies at the foundation of marriage and the family, which is the first school where we learn to appreciate our talents and those of others, and where we begin to acquire the art of living together. For most of us, the family is the principal place in which we begin to 'breathe' values and ideals, as we develop our full capacity for virtue and charity. At the same time, as we know, in families tensions arise: between egoism and altruism, between reason and passion, between immediate desires and long-term goals, and so on. But families also provide the environment in which these tensions are resolved: this is important. When we speak of complementarity between man and woman in this context, we must not confuse the term with the simplistic idea that all the roles and relationships of both sexes are confined to a single and static model. Complementarity assumes many forms, since every man and every woman brings their personal contribution – personal richness, their own charisma – to the marriage and to the upbringing of their children. Thus, complementarity becomes a great treasure. It is not only an asset but is also a thing of beauty.

Marriage and the family are in crisis today. We now live in a culture of the temporary, in which more and more people reject marriage as a public obligation. This revolution of customs and morals has often waved 'the flag of freedom', but it has, in reality, brought spiritual and material devastation to countless human beings, especially the poorest and most vulnerable. It is ever more evident that the decline of the culture of marriage is associated with increased poverty and a host of other social ills that disproportionately affect women, children and the elderly. It is always they who suffer the most in this crisis.

The crisis of the family has produced a human ecological crisis, for social environments, like natural environments, need protection. Although humanity has come to understand the need to address the conditions that threaten our natural environment, we have been slow – we have been slow in our culture, even in our Catholic culture – we have been slow to recognise that even our social environments are at risk. It is therefore essential that we foster a new human ecology and make it move forward.

It is necessary to insist on the fundamental pillars that govern a nation: its intangible assets. The family is the foundation of co-existence and a guarantee against social fragmentation. Children have a right to grow up in a family with a father and a mother capable of creating a suitable environment for the child's growth and emotional development. This is why, in the Apostolic Exhortation *Evangelii Gaudium*, I stressed the 'indispensable' contribution of marriage to society, a contribution which 'transcends the feelings and momentary needs of the couple' (n. 66). And this is why I am grateful to you for the emphasis that your colloquium has placed on the benefits that marriage can provide children, the spouses themselves, and society.

In these days, as you reflect on the complementarity between man and woman, I urge you to emphasise yet another truth about marriage: that the permanent commitment to solidarity, fidelity and fruitful love responds to the deepest longings of the human heart. Let us think especially of the young people who represent our future: it is important that they should not let the harmful mentality of the temporary affect them, but rather that they be revolutionaries with the courage to seek strong and lasting love, in other words, to go against the current: this must be done. I would like to say one thing about this: we must not fall into the trap of being limited by ideological concepts. The family is an anthropological fact, and consequently a social, cultural fact, etc. We cannot qualify it with ideological concepts which are compelling at only one moment in history, and then decline. Today there can be no talk of the *conservative family* or the *progressive family*: family is family! Do not allow yourselves to be qualified by this, or by other ideological concepts. The family has a force of its own.

5

The Cross and the Resurrection of Jesus

He turned himself in for me

With Palm Sunday starts Holy Week – the heart of the whole liturgical year – in which we accompany Jesus in his Passion, death and resurrection.

But what does living Holy Week mean to us? What does following Jesus on his journey to Calvary, on his way to the cross and the resurrection mean? In his earthly mission Jesus walked the roads of the Holy Land; he called 12 simple people to stay with him, to share his journey and to continue his mission. He chose them from among the people full of faith in God's promises. He spoke to all without distinction: the great and the lowly, the rich young man and the poor widow, the powerful and the weak; he brought God's mercy and forgiveness; he healed, he comforted, he understood; he gave hope; he brought to all the presence of God who cares for every man and every woman, just as a good father and a good mother care for each one of their children. God does not wait for us to go to him but it is he who moves towards us, without calculation, without quantification.

That is what God is like. He always takes the first step, he comes towards us. Jesus lived the daily reality of the most ordinary people: he was moved as he faced the crowd that seemed like a flock without a shepherd; he wept before the sorrow that Martha and Mary felt at the death of their brother, Lazarus; he called a publican to be his disciple; he also suffered betrayal by a friend. In him God has given us the certitude that he is with us, he is among us. 'Foxes', he, Jesus, said, 'have holes, and birds of the air have nests, but the Son of man has nowhere to lay his head' (Matt. 8:20). Jesus has no house, because his house is the people, it is we who are his dwelling place; his mission is to open God's doors to all, to be the presence of God's love.

In Holy Week we live the crowning moment of this journey, of this plan of love that runs through the entire history of the relations between God and humanity. Jesus enters Jerusalem to take his last step with which he sums up the whole of his existence. He gives himself without reserve, he keeps nothing for himself, not even life. At the Last Supper, with his friends, he breaks the bread and passes the cup round 'for us'. The Son of God offers himself to us, he puts his body and his Blood into our hands, so as to be with us always, to dwell among us. And in the Garden of Olives, and likewise in the trial before Pilate, he puts up no resistance, he gives himself; he is the Suffering Servant, foretold by Isaiah, who empties himself, even unto death (cf. Isa. 53:12).

Jesus does not experience this love that leads to his sacrifice passively or as a fatal destiny. He does not of course conceal his deep human distress as he faces a violent death, but with absolute trust commends himself to the Father. Jesus gave himself up to death voluntarily in order to reciprocate the love of God the Father, in perfect union with his will, to demonstrate his love for us. On the cross Jesus 'loved me and gave himself for me' (Gal. 2:20). Each one of us can say, 'He loved me and gave himself for me.' Each one can say this 'for me'.

What is the meaning of all this for us? It means that this is my, your and our road too. Living Holy Week, following Jesus not only with the emotion of the heart; living Holy Week, following Jesus means learning to come out of ourselves – as I said last Sunday – in order to go to meet others, to go towards the outskirts of existence, to be the first to take a step towards our brothers and our sisters, especially those who are the most distant, those who are forgotten, those who are most in need of understanding, comfort and help. There is such a great need to bring the living presence of Jesus, merciful and full of love!

Living Holy Week means entering ever more deeply into the logic of God, into the logic of the cross, which is not primarily that of suffering and death, but rather that of love and of the gift of self which brings life. It means entering into the logic of the gospel. Following and accompanying Christ, staying with him, demands 'coming out of ourselves', requires us to be outgoing; to come out of ourselves, out of a dreary way of living faith that has become a habit, out of the temptation to withdraw into our own plans which end by shutting out God's creative action. God came out of himself to come among us, he pitched his tent among us to bring to us his mercy that saves and gives hope. Nor must we be satisfied with staying in the pen of the 99 sheep if we want to follow him and to remain with him; we too must 'go out' with him to seek the lost sheep, the one that has strayed the furthest. Be sure to remember: let us come out of ourselves, just as Jesus, just as God came out of himself in Jesus and Jesus came out of himself for all of us.

Someone might say to me, 'But, Father, I don't have time', 'I have so many things to do', 'It's difficult', 'What can I do with my feebleness and my sins, with so many things?' We are often satisfied with a few prayers, with a distracted and sporadic participation in Sunday Mass, with a few charitable acts; but we do not have the courage 'to come out' to bring Christ to others. We are a bit like St Peter. As soon as Jesus speaks of his Passion, death and resurrection, of the gift of himself, of love for all, the apostle takes him aside and reproaches him. What Jesus says upsets his plans, seems unacceptable, threatens the security he had built for himself, his idea of the Messiah. And Jesus looks at his disciples and addresses to Peter what may possibly be the harshest words in the Gospels: 'Get behind me Satan! You are thinking not as God thinks, but as human beings do'(Mark 8:33 NJB).

God always thinks with mercy: do not forget this. God always thinks mercifully. He is the merciful Father! God thinks like the father waiting for the son and goes to meet him, he spots him coming when he is still far off ... What does this mean? That he went every day to see if his son was coming home: this is our merciful Father. It indicates that he was waiting for him with longing on the terrace of his house. God thinks like the Samaritan who did not pass by the unfortunate man, pitying him or looking at him from the other side of the road, but helped him without asking for anything in return; without asking whether he was a Jew, a pagan or a Samaritan, whether he was rich or poor – he asked for nothing. He went to help him: God is like this. God thinks like the shepherd who lays down his life in order to defend and save his sheep.

Holy Week is a time of grace which the Lord gives us to *open the doors* of our heart, of our life, of our parishes – what a pity so many parishes are closed! – of the movements, of the associations; and 'to come out' in order to meet others, to make ourselves close, to bring them the light and joy of our faith. To come out always! And to do so with God's love and tenderness, with respect and with patience, knowing that God takes our hands, our feet, our heart, and guides them and makes all our actions fruitful.

Learning how to embrace the cross

Jesus enters Jerusalem. The crowd of disciples accompanies him in festive mood, their garments are stretched out before him, there is talk of the miracles he has accomplished, and loud praises are heard: 'Blessed is the King who comes in the name of the Lord. Peace in heaven and glory in the highest!' (Luke 19:38).

Crowds, celebrating, praise, blessing, peace: joy fills the air. Jesus has awakened great hopes, especially in the hearts of the simple, the humble, the poor, the forgotten, those who do not matter in the eyes of the world. He understands human sufferings, he has shown the face of God's mercy, and he has bent down to heal body and soul.

This is Jesus. This is his heart which looks to all of us, to our sicknesses, to our sins. The love of Jesus is great. And thus he enters Jerusalem, with this love, and looks at us. It is a beautiful scene, full of light – the light of the love of Jesus, the love of his heart – of joy, of celebration.

At the beginning of Mass, we too repeated it. We waved our palms, our olive branches. We too welcomed Jesus; we too expressed our joy at accompanying him, at knowing him to be close, present in us and among us as a friend, a brother, and also as a king, that is, a shining beacon for our lives. Jesus is God, but he lowered himself to walk with us. He is our friend, our brother. He illumines our path here. And in this way we have welcomed him today. And here the first word that I wish to say to you: *joy*!

Do not be men and women of sadness: a Christian can never be sad! Never give way to discouragement! Ours is not a joy born of having many possessions, but from having encountered a Person: Jesus, in our midst. It is born from knowing that with him we are never alone, even at difficult moments, even when our life's journey comes up against problems and obstacles that seem insurmountable, and there are so many of them! And in this moment the enemy, the devil, comes, often disguised as an angel, and slyly speaks his word to us. Do not listen to him! Let us follow Jesus! We accompany, we follow Jesus, but above all we know that he accompanies us and carries us on his shoulders. This is our joy, this is the hope that we must bring to this world. Please do not let yourselves be robbed of hope! Do not let hope be stolen! The hope that Jesus gives us.

The second word. Why does Jesus enter Jerusalem? Or better: how does Jesus enter Jerusalem? The crowds acclaim him as king. And he does not deny it, he does not tell them to be silent (cf. Luke 19:39–40). But what kind of a king is Jesus? Let us take a look at him: he is riding on a donkey, he is not accompanied by a court, he is not surrounded by an army as a symbol of power. He is received by humble people, simple folk who have the sense to see something more in Jesus; they have that sense of the faith which says, here is the Saviour. Jesus does not enter the Holy City to receive the honours reserved to earthly kings, to the powerful, to rulers; he enters to be scourged, insulted and abused, as Isaiah foretold in the first reading (cf. Isa. 50:6). He enters to receive a crown of thorns, a staff, a purple robe: his kingship becomes an object of derision. He enters to climb Calvary, carrying his burden of wood. And this brings us to the second word: *cross*.

Jesus enters Jerusalem in order to die on the cross. And it is precisely here that his kingship shines forth in godly fashion: his royal throne is the wood of the cross! It reminds me of what Benedict XVI said to the cardinals: you are princes, but of a king crucified. That is the throne of Jesus. Jesus takes it upon himself … Why the cross? Because Jesus takes upon himself the evil, the filth, the sin of the world, including the sin of all of us, and he cleanses it, he cleanses it with his blood, with the mercy and the love of God. Let us look around: how many wounds are inflicted upon humanity by evil! Wars, violence, economic conflicts that hit the weakest, greed for money that you can't take with you and have to leave. When we were small, our grandmother used to say, a shroud has no pocket. Love of power, corruption, divisions, crimes against human life and against creation! And – as each one of us knows and is aware – our personal sins: our failures in love and respect towards God, towards our neighbour and towards the whole of creation. Jesus on the cross feels the whole weight of the evil, and with the force of God's love he conquers it, he defeats it with his resurrection. This is the good that Jesus does for us on the throne of the cross. Christ's cross embraced with love never leads to sadness, but to joy, to the joy of having been saved and of doing a little of what he did on the day of his death.

[…] For 28 years Palm Sunday has been World Youth Day! This is our third word: *youth*! Dear young people […] I think of you celebrating around Jesus, waving your olive branches. I think of you crying out his name and expressing your joy at being with him! You have an important part in the celebration of faith! You bring us the joy of faith and you tell us that we must live the faith with a young heart, always: a young heart, even at the age of 70 or 80. Dear young people! With Christ, the heart never grows old! Yet all of us, all of you know very well that the king whom we follow and who accompanies us is very special: he is a king who loves even to the cross and who teaches us to serve and to love. And you are not ashamed of his cross! On the contrary, you embrace it, because you have understood that it is in giving ourselves, in giving ourselves, in emerging from ourselves that we have true joy and that, with his love, God conquered evil. You carry the pilgrim cross through all the continents, along the highways of the world! You carry it in response to Jesus' call: 'Go, make disciples of all nations' (Matt. 28:19).

Together in pain and love

We have come here today [Way of the Cross, Copacabana] to accompany Jesus on his journey of sorrow and love, the Way of the Cross, which is one of the most intense moments of World Youth Day. At the end of the Holy Year of Redemption, Blessed John Paul II chose to entrust the cross to you, young people, asking you 'to carry it throughout the world as a symbol of Christ's love for humanity, and announce to everyone that only in the death and resurrection of Christ can we find salvation and redemption' (Address to Young People, 22 April 1984). Since then, the World Youth Day cross has travelled to every continent and through a variety of human situations. It is, as it were, almost 'steeped' in the life experiences of the countless young people who have seen it and carried it. Dear brothers and sisters, no one can approach and touch the cross of Jesus without leaving something of himself or herself there, and without bringing something of the cross of Jesus into his or her own life. I have three questions that I hope will echo in your hearts this evening as you walk beside Jesus: What have you left on the cross, dear young people of Brazil, during these two years that it has been criss-crossing your great country? What has the cross of Jesus left for you, in each one of you? Finally, what does this cross teach us?

According to an ancient Roman tradition, while fleeing the city during the persecutions of Nero, St Peter saw Jesus who was travelling in the opposite direction, that is, towards the city, and asked him in amazement, 'Lord, where are you going?' Jesus' response was, 'I am going to Rome to be crucified again.' At that moment, Peter understood that he had to follow the Lord with courage, to the very end. But he also realised that he would never be alone on the journey; Jesus, who had loved him even unto death, would always be with him. Jesus, with his cross, walks with us and takes upon himself our fears, our problems, and our sufferings, even those which are deepest and most painful. With the cross, Jesus unites himself to the silence of the victims of violence, those who can no longer cry out, especially the innocent and the defenceless; with the cross, he is united to families in trouble, and those who mourn the tragic loss of their children, as in the case of the 242 young victims of the fire in the city of Santa Maria at the beginning of this year.

On the cross, Jesus is united with every person who suffers from hunger in a world which, on the other hand, permits itself the luxury of throwing away tons of food every day; on the cross, Jesus is united to the many mothers and fathers who suffer as they see their children become victims of drug-induced euphoria; on the cross, Jesus is united with those who are persecuted for their religion, for their beliefs or simply for the colour of their skin; on the cross, Jesus is united with so many young people who have lost faith in political institutions, because they see in them only selfishness and corruption; he unites himself with those young people who have lost faith in the Church, or even in God, because of the counter-witness of Christians and ministers of the gospel. How our inconsistencies make Jesus suffer!

The cross of Christ bears the suffering and the sin of humankind, including our own. Jesus accepts all this with open arms, bearing on his shoulders our crosses and saying to us, 'Have courage! You do not carry your cross alone! I carry it with you. I have overcome death and I have come to give you hope, to give you life' (cf. John 3:16).

Now we can answer the second question: What has the cross given to those who have gazed upon it and to those who have touched it? What has the cross left in each one of us? You see, it gives us a treasure that no one else can give: the certainty of the faithful love which God has for us. A love so great that it enters into our sin and forgives it, enters into our suffering and gives us the strength to bear it. It is a love which enters into death to conquer it and to save us. The cross of Christ contains all the love of God; there we find his immeasurable mercy. This is a love in which we can place all our trust, in which we can believe. Dear young people, let us entrust ourselves to Jesus, let us give ourselves over to him (cf. *Lumen Fidei*, 16), because he never disappoints anyone! Only in Christ crucified and risen can we find salvation and redemption. With him, evil, suffering and death do not have the last word, because he gives us hope and life: he has transformed the cross from being an instrument of hate, defeat and death to being a sign of love, victory, triumph and life.

The first name given to Brazil was 'The Land of the Holy Cross'. The cross of Christ was planted five centuries ago not only on the shores of this country, but also in the history, the hearts and the lives of the people of Brazil and elsewhere. The suffering Christ is keenly felt here, as one of us who shares our journey even to the end. There is no cross, big or small, in our life which the Lord does not share with us.

But the cross of Christ invites us also to allow ourselves to be smitten by his love, teaching us always to look upon others with mercy and tenderness, especially those who suffer, who are in need of help, who need a word or a concrete action; the cross invites us to step outside ourselves to meet them and to extend a hand to them. How many times have we seen them in the *Way of the Cross*, how many times have they accompanied Jesus on the way to Calvary: Pilate, Simon of Cyrene, Mary, the women … Today I ask you: which of them do you want to be? Do you want to be like Pilate, who did not have the courage to go against the tide to save Jesus' life, and instead washed his hands? Tell me: are you one of those who wash their hands, who feign ignorance and look the other way? Or are you like Simon of Cyrene, who helped Jesus to carry that heavy wood, or like Mary and the other women, who were not afraid to accompany Jesus all the way to the end, with love and tenderness? And you, who do you want to be? Like Pilate? Like Simon? Like Mary? Jesus is looking at you now and is asking you, 'Do you want to help me carry the cross?' Brothers and sisters, with all the strength of your youth, how will you respond to him?

Dear friends, let us bring to Christ's cross our joys, our sufferings and our failures. There we will find a heart that is open to us and understands us, forgives us, loves us and calls us to bear this love in our lives, to love each person, each brother and sister, with the same love.

Before the sufferings of my Lord

'He came out and went … to the Mount of Olives; and the disciples followed him' (Luke 22:39). At the hour which God had appointed to save humanity from its enslavement to sin, Jesus came here, to Gethsemane, to the foot of the Mount of Olives. We now find ourselves [meeting with priests, at the Church of Gethsemane] in this holy place, a place sanctified by the prayer of Jesus, by his agony, by his sweating of blood, and above all by his 'yes' to the loving will of the Father. We dread in some sense to approach what Jesus went through at that hour; we tread softly as we enter that inner space where the destiny of the world was decided.

In that hour, Jesus felt the need to pray and to have with him his disciples, his friends, those who had followed him and shared most closely in his mission. But [...] at Gethsemane, following him became difficult and uncertain; they were overcome by doubt, weariness and fright. As the events of Jesus' Passion rapidly unfolded, the disciples would adopt different attitudes before the Master: attitudes of closeness, distance, hesitation.

[...] Each of us – bishops, priests, consecrated persons, and seminarians – might do well to ask: Who am I, before the sufferings of my Lord?

Am I among those who, when Jesus asks them to keep watch with him, fall asleep instead, and rather than praying, seek to escape, refusing to face reality?

Or do I see myself in those who fled out of fear, who abandoned the Master at the most tragic hour in his earthly life?

Is there perhaps duplicity in me, like that of the one who sold our Lord for 30 pieces of silver, who once called Jesus' 'friend', and yet ended up by betraying him?

Do I see myself in those who drew back and denied him, like Peter? Shortly before, he had promised Jesus that he would follow him even unto death (cf. Luke 22:33); but then, put to the test and assailed by fear, he swore he did not know him.

Am I like those who began planning to go about their lives without him, like the two disciples on the road to Emmaus, foolish and slow of heart to believe the words of the prophets (cf. Luke 24:25)?

Or, thanks be to God, do I find myself among those who remained faithful to the end, like the Virgin Mary and the apostle John? On Golgotha, when everything seemed bleak and all hope seemed pointless, only love proved stronger than death. The love of the Mother and the beloved disciple made them stay at the foot of the cross, sharing in the pain of Jesus, to the very end.

Do I recognise myself in those who imitated their Master to the point of martyrdom, testifying that he was everything to them, the incomparable strength sustaining their mission and the ultimate horizon of their lives?

Jesus' friendship with us, his faithfulness and his mercy, are a priceless gift which encourages us to follow him trustingly, notwithstanding our failures, our mistakes, also our betrayals.

But the Lord's goodness does not dispense us from the need for vigilance before the Tempter, before sin, before the evil and the betrayal which can enter even into the religious and priestly life. We are all exposed to sin, to evil, to betrayal. We are fully conscious of the disproportion between the grandeur of God's call and of own littleness, between the sublimity of the mission and the reality of our human weakness. Yet the Lord in his great goodness and his infinite mercy always takes us by the hand lest we drown in the sea of our fears and anxieties. He is ever at our side, he never abandons us. And so, let us not be overwhelmed by fear or disheartened, but with courage and confidence let us press forward in our journey and in our mission.

You, dear brothers and sisters, are called to follow the Lord with joy in this holy land! It is a gift and also a responsibility. Your presence here is extremely important; the whole Church is grateful to you and she sustains you by her prayers. From this holy place, I wish to extend my heartfelt greetings to all Christians in Jerusalem: I would like to assure them that I remember them affectionately and that I pray for them, being well aware of the difficulties they experience in this city. I urge them to be courageous witnesses of the Passion of the Lord but also of his resurrection, with joy and hope.

Let us imitate the Virgin Mary and St John, and stand by all those crosses where Jesus continues to be crucified. This is how the Lord calls us to follow him: this is the path, there is no other!

'Whoever serves me must follow me, and where I am, there will my servant be also' (John 12:26).

From the slavery of sin to the freedom of love

What a joy it is for me to announce this message: Christ is risen! I would like it to go out to every house and every family, especially where the suffering is greatest, in hospitals, in prisons …

Most of all, I would like it to enter every heart, for it is there that God wants to sow this good news: Jesus is risen, there is hope for you, you are no longer in the power of sin, of evil! Love has triumphed, mercy has been victorious! The mercy of God always triumphs!

We too, like the women who were Jesus' disciples, who went to the tomb and found it empty, may wonder what this event means (cf. Luke 24:4). What does it mean that Jesus is risen? It means that the love of God is stronger than evil and death itself; it means that the love of God can transform our lives and let those desert places in our hearts bloom. The love God can do this!

This same love for which the Son of God became human and followed the way of humility and self-giving to the very end, down to hell – to the abyss of separation from God – this same merciful love has flooded with light the dead body of Jesus, has transfigured it, has made it pass into eternal life. Jesus did not return to his former life, to earthly life, but entered into the glorious life of God and he entered there with our humanity, opening us to a future of hope.

This is what Easter is: it is the exodus, the passage of human beings from slavery to sin and evil to the freedom of love and goodness. Because God is life, life alone, and we are his glory: the living person (cf. Irenaeus, *Adversus Haereses*, 4,20,5–7).

Christ died and rose once for all, and for everyone, but the power of the resurrection, this passover from slavery to evil to the freedom of goodness, must be accomplished in every age, in our concrete existence, in our everyday lives. How many deserts, even today, do human beings need to cross! Above all, the desert within, when we have no love for God or neighbour, when we fail to realise that we are guardians of all that the Creator has given us and continues to give us. God's mercy can make even the driest land become a garden, can restore life to dry bones (cf. Ez 37:1–14).

So this is the invitation which I address to everyone: let us accept the grace of Christ's resurrection! Let us be renewed by God's mercy, let us be loved by Jesus, let us enable the power of his love to transform our lives too; and let us become agents of this mercy, channels through which God can water the earth, protect all creation and make justice and peace flourish.

And so we ask the risen Jesus, who turns death into life, to change hatred into love, vengeance into forgiveness, war into peace. Yes, Christ is our peace, and through him we implore peace for all the world.

Peace for the Middle East, and particularly between Israelis and Palestinians, who struggle to find the road of agreement, that they may willingly and courageously resume negotiations to end a conflict that has lasted all too long. Peace in Iraq, that every act of violence may end, and above all for dear Syria, for its people torn by conflict and for the many refugees who await help and comfort. How much blood has been shed! And how much suffering must there still be before a political solution to the crisis will be found?

Peace for Africa, still the scene of violent conflicts. In Mali, may unity and stability be restored; in Nigeria, where attacks sadly continue, gravely threatening the lives of many innocent people, and where great numbers of persons, including children, are held hostage by terrorist groups. Peace in the east of the Democratic Republic of Congo, and in the Central African Republic, where many have been forced to leave their homes and continue to live in fear.

Peace in Asia, above all on the Korean peninsula: may disagreements be overcome and a renewed spirit of reconciliation grow.

Peace in the whole world, still divided by greed looking for easy gain, wounded by the selfishness which threatens human life and the family, selfishness that continues in human trafficking, the most extensive form of slavery in this twenty-first century; human trafficking is the most extensive form of slavery in this twenty-first century! Peace to the whole world, torn apart by violence linked to drug trafficking and by the iniquitous exploitation of natural resources! Peace to this our Earth! May the risen Jesus bring comfort to the victims of natural disasters and make us responsible guardians of creation.

Lent without Easter

There are Christians whose lives seem like Lent without Easter. I realise of course that joy is not expressed the same way at all times in life, especially at moments of great difficulty. Joy adapts and changes, but it always endures, even as a flicker of light born of our personal certainty that, when everything is said and done, we are infinitely loved. I understand the grief of people who have to endure great suffering, yet slowly but surely we all have to let the joy of faith slowly revive as a quiet yet firm trust, even amid the greatest distress: 'My soul is bereft of peace; I have forgotten what happiness is ... But this I call to mind, and therefore I have hope: the steadfast love of the Lord never ceases, his mercies never come to an end; they are new every morning. Great is your faithfulness ... It is good that one should wait quietly for the salvation of the Lord' (Lam. 3:17, 21–23, 26).

Sometimes we are tempted to find excuses and complain, acting as if we could only be happy if a thousand conditions were met. To some extent this is because our 'technological society has succeeded in multiplying occasions of pleasure, yet has found it very difficult to engender joy' (Paul VI, Apostolic Exhortation, *Gaudete in Domino*, 8). I can say that the most beautiful and natural expressions of joy which I have seen in my life were in poor people who had little to hold on to. I also think of the real joy shown by others who, even amid pressing professional obligations, were able to preserve, in detachment and simplicity, a heart full of faith. In their own way, all these instances of joy flow from the infinite love of God, who has revealed himself to us in Jesus Christ. I never tire of repeating those words of Benedict XVI which take us to the very heart of the gospel: 'Being a Christian is not the result of an ethical choice or a lofty idea, but the encounter with an event, a person, which gives life a new horizon and a decisive direction' (Encyclical, *Deus caritas est*, 1).

Thanks solely to this encounter – or renewed encounter – with God's love, which blossoms into an enriching friendship, we are liberated from our narrowness and self-absorption. We become fully human when we become more than human, when we let God bring us beyond ourselves in order to attain the fullest truth of our being. Here we find the source and inspiration of all our efforts at evangelization. For if we have received the love which restores meaning to our lives, how can we fail to share that love with others?

In the joy of the Risen One

Happy Easter! *Cristòs anèsti*! – *Alethòs anèsti*! Christ is risen! – He is risen indeed! He is among us, here, in the Square! This week we can continue to exchange Easter greetings, as though it were one single day. It is the great day which the Lord has made.

The dominant sentiment that shines forth from the gospel accounts of the resurrection is joy full of wonder, but a great wonder! Joy that comes from within! And in the Liturgy we relive the state of mind of the disciples over the news which the women had brought: Jesus is risen! We have seen him!

Let us allow this experience which is inscribed in the gospel also to be imprinted in our hearts and shine forth from our lives. Let us allow the joyous wonder of Easter Sunday to shine forth in our thoughts, glances, behaviour, gestures and words ... If only we were so luminous! But this is not just cosmetic. It comes from within, from a heart immersed in the source of this joy, like that of Mary Magdalene, who wept over the loss of her Lord and could hardly believe her eyes seeing him risen. Whoever experiences this becomes a witness of the resurrection, for in a certain sense he himself has risen, she herself has risen. He or she is then capable of carrying a 'ray' of light of the Risen One into various situations: to those that are happy, making them more beautiful by preserving them from egoism; to those that are painful, bringing serenity and hope.

Over the course of this week it will do us good to take up the Book of the Gospel and read those chapters which speak about Jesus' resurrection. It will really do us good! To take up the Book, look for the chapter and read it. It will also benefit us this week to think about the joy of Mary, the Mother of Jesus. Just as her pain was intimate enough to pierce her soul, so too her joy was also intimate and deep, and the disciples were able to draw from it. Having passed through the experience of the death and resurrection of her Son, seen in faith as the supreme expression of God's love, Mary's heart became a font of peace, consolation, hope and mercy. All of the prerogatives of our Mother derive from this, from her participation in Jesus' paschal mystery. From Friday until Sunday morning she did not lose hope: we contemplated the sorrowful Mother but, at the same time, the Mother full of hope. She, who is the

Mother of all of the disciples, the Mother of the Church, is the Mother of hope.

Walking towards the kingdom

In presenting the Church to the men and women of our time, the Second Vatican Council kept well in mind a fundamental truth, one we should never forget: the Church is not a static reality, inert, an end in herself, but is on a continual journey through history, towards that ultimate and marvellous end that is the kingdom of heaven, of which the Church on earth is the seed and the beginning (cf. Dogmatic Constitution on the Church, *Lumen Gentium*, n. 5). When we turn to this horizon, we discover that our imagination falls short, hardly able to intuit the splendour of a mystery which surpasses our senses. And several questions spontaneously rise up in us: when will that final step happen? What will the new dimension which the Church enters be like? What will become of humanity then? And of creation around us? But these questions are not new, the disciples had already asked Jesus about them at that time: 'When will this come to pass? When will the Spirit triumph over creation, over creatures, over everything ...?' These are human questions, time-old questions. And we too are asking these questions.

The Conciliar Constitution *Gaudium et Spes* faced with these questions that forever resonate in the hearts of men and women, states:

> We do not know the time for the consummation of the earth and of humanity, nor do we know how all things will be transformed. As deformed by sin, the shape of this world will pass away; but we are taught that God is preparing a new dwelling place and a new earth where justice will abide, and whose blessedness will answer and surpass all the longings for peace which spring up in the human heart. (n. 39)

This is the Church's destination: it is, as the Bible says, the 'new Jerusalem', 'Paradise'. More than a place, it is a 'state' of soul in which our deepest hopes are fulfilled in superabundance and our being, as creatures and as children of God, reach their full maturity. We will finally be clothed in the joy, peace and love of God, completely, without any limit, and we will come face to face with Him! (cf. 1 Cor. 13:12). It is beautiful to think of this, to think of heaven. We will all be there together. It is beautiful, it gives strength to the soul.

In this perspective, it is good to grasp the kind of continuity and deep communion there is between the Church in heaven and that which is still a pilgrim on earth. Those who already live in the sight of God can indeed sustain us and intercede for us, pray for us. On the other hand, we too are always invited to offer up good works, prayer and the Eucharist itself in order to alleviate the tribulation of souls still awaiting never-ending beatitude. Yes, because in the Christian perspective the distinction is not between who is dead and who is not, but between who is in Christ and who is not! This is the point of determination, what is truly decisive for our salvation and for our happiness.

At the same time, sacred Scripture teaches us that the fulfilment of this marvellous plan cannot but involve everything that surrounds us and came from the heart and mind of God. The apostle Paul says it explicitly, when he says that 'Creation itself will be set free from its bondage to decay and obtain the glorious liberty of the children of God' (Rom. 8:21). Other texts utilise the image of a 'new heaven' and a 'new earth' (cf. 2 Pet. 3:13; Rev. 21:1), in the sense that the whole universe will be renewed and will be freed once and for all from every trace of evil and from death itself. What lies ahead is the fulfilment of a transformation that in reality is already happening, beginning with the death and resurrection of Christ. Hence, it is the new creation; it is not, therefore, the annihilation of the cosmos and of everything around us, but the bringing of all things into the fullness of being, of truth and of beauty. This is the design that God, the Father, Son and Holy Spirit, willed from eternity to realise and is realising.

Dear friends, when we think of this magnificent reality awaiting us, we become aware of how marvellous a gift it is to belong to the Church which bears in writing the highest of vocations! So, let us ask the Virgin Mary, Mother of the Church, to keep constant watch over our journey and help us to be, as she is, a joyful sign of trust and hope among our brothers and sisters.

Key Dates in Pope Francis's Life

1936 *17 December.* Jorge Mario Bergoglio was born in Buenos Aires to a family, originally from Asti (Italy), who migrated to Argentina. Mario, his father, was an accountant in the railway company; Regina Sivori, his mother, was a housewife. Jorge was the first of five children: Oscar, Marta, Alberto and María Elena.

1957 After achieving his diploma in chemistry, he chose to become a priest and started seminary in Villa Devoto.

1958 *11 March.* Started his novitiate at the Society of Jesus and, two years later (12 March 1960), took his first vows.

1963 After completing his humanistic studies in Santiago in Chile, he went back to Argentina, where he earned his philosophy degree at San José College in San Miguel.

1964 –66 Taught literature and psychology, first in Santa Fé and then in Buenos Aires.

1969 *13 December.* Ordained priest.

1970 Finished his theological studies and graduated at San José College.

1973 *22 April.* He made his perpetual profession.

31 July. After being consultor, he became provincial superior of the Argentinean Jesuits.

1980 Appointed Rector of San José College. Until 1986 he worked in this position and then stepped down to study theology in Germany and to do research on Romano Guardini for his PhD thesis. His studies in Germany were interrupted by a summons from his superiors in Argentina to take up higher positions. As a priest he ministered in a parish in Córdoba.

1992 *20 May*. After serving for several years as spiritual director and confessor, he was appointed Auxiliary Bishop of Buenos Aires by John Paul II. He worked closely with Cardinal Antonio Quarracino, from whom he received episcopal ordination (27 June). As his motto he chose 'Miserando atque eligendo' ('Having mercy, he chose him') and in his coat of arms he inserted the Christogram *IHS*, symbol of the Society of Jesus.

1993 *21 December*. Appointed Vicar General of the Archdiocese.

1997 *3 June*. Promoted to Coadjutor Archbishop of Buenos Aires. A year later, when Cardinal Quarracino died, he succeeded him in leading the archdiocese (28 February) and also became the Primate of Argentina.

2001 *21 February*. Created a cardinal by John Paul II.

2005 Took part in the Conclave electing Benedict XVI.

2013 *11 February*. Benedict XVI announced he would relinquish the Petrine ministry at the end of the month.

13 March. Elected the new Supreme Pontiff, choosing the name Francis, the first Latin American Pope, the first Jesuit Pope and the first to take the name Francis.

7 April. Took up his seat as Bishop of Rome on the 'Cathedra romana'.

24 June. Created a pontifical commission to investigate on the Institute for Works of Religion (the Vatican bank).

29 June. First encyclical, *Lumen fidei* published, thus completing the document Benedict XVI bequeathed to him.

8 July. Took an historical visit to the island of Lampedusa.

22 –29 July. Took part in the World Youth Day in Rio de Janeiro, Brazil.

22 September. Pastoral visit to Cagliari.

28 September. Established the 'Council of Cardinals', whose tasks are to advise Francis on ruling the Universal Church and to start a reorganisation of the Apostolic Constitution *Pastor bonus* regarding the role of the Roman Curia.

4 October. Pastoral visit to Assisi.

24 November. Apostolic Exhortation *Evangelii gaudium* published.

2014   *22 February.* Summoned the Consistory for the creation of new cardinals.

27 April. Canonisation of the Blessed John XXIII and John Paul II.

24–26 May. Pilgrimage in the Holy Land.

June–July. Pastoral visits to Cassano all'Jonio (21 June), to the dioceses of Campobasso-Boiano, Isernia-Venafro (5 July) and Caserta (26 July).

13–18 August. Apostolic trip to Korea, on the occasion of the VI Asiatic youth day.

21 September. Apostolic trip to Albania.

19 October. Solemn beatification of Paul VI.

25 November. Visit to the Council of Europe and to the European Parliament.

28–30 November. Apostolic trip to Turkey.

2015 *12–19 January.* Apostolic trip to Sri Lanka and the Philippines.

14–15 February. Summoned the Consistory for the creation of new cardinals.

List of Sources

1. *The Chains of the World*

    The desire for possession: Angelus, 2 March 2014 (www.vatican.va).

    The false happiness of the transient: Address to the seminarians, 6 July 2013 (www.vatican.va).

    The sterile disease of pessimism: *Evangelii Gaudium,* 24 November 2013, nos. 84–86 (www.vatican.va).

    The factory of destruction: Homily at Verano Cemetery, 1 November 2014 (www.vatican.va).

    The paradox of abundance: Speech at FAO in Rome, 20 November 2014 (www.vatican.va).

    The functioning of extreme consumerism: Speech at the European Parliament, 25 November 2014 (www.vatican.va).

    The temptations of the pastor: Speech at the General Assembly of Episcopal Conference of Italy, 19 May 2014 (www.vatican.va).

    Do not take over the vineyard: Homily, 5 October 2014 (www.vatican.va).

2. *Changing the Heart*

    We are creatures, we are not God: Homily at Santa Sabina basilica, 5 March 2014 (www.vatican.va).

    Listening to the word of Jesus: Angelus, 16 March 2014 (www.vatican.va).

The courage of looking inside one's self: Angelus, 23 March 2014 (www.vatican.va).

The appeal to conversion: Homily, 28 March 2014 (www.vatican.va).

Where is my heart?: Homily on Palm Sunday, 13 April 2014 (www.vatican.va).

Opening up to the light: Angelus, 30 March 2014 (www.vatican.va).

The alphabet of the priestly spirit: General Audience, 12 November 2014 (www.vatican.va).

3. *The Walk of a Christian Life*

Lead the way: Address to the adult movement of Italian Catholic scouts, 8 November 2014 (www.vatican.va).

The power of prayers: Angelus, 20 October 2013 (www.vatican.va).

To obey the commandments: Video message to the participants to the initiative 'Ten squares for ten commandments', 8 June 2013 (www.vatican.va).

Trust God's patience: Homily at St John in Lateran Basilica, 7 April 2013 (www.vatican.va).

The courage of creativity: Speech at the Assembly of the Focolare Movement, 26 September 2014 (www.vatican.va).

With you we will make great things: Homily at the holy Mass for the conferral of the sacrament of confirmation, 28 April 2013 (www.vatican.va).

Let us go forward on the path to holiness: General Audience, 19 November 2014 (www.vatican.va).

4. *On the Streets of Humanity*

Members of a Mother Church: General Audience, 3 September 2014 (www.vatican.va).

In the school of mercy: General Audience, 10 September 2014 (www.vatican.va).

Offering our gifts to others: General Audience, 1 October 2014 (www.vatican.va).

Listening to the cry of the poor: Address to the participants in the World Meeting of Popular Movements, 28 October 2014 (www.vatican.va).

The challenge of a family: Speech at the General Assembly of the Council of the Episcopal Conferences of Europe, 3 October 2014 (www.vatican.va).

For the culture of marriage: Speech at the International Colloquium sponsored by the Congregation for the Doctrine of the Faith, 17 November 2014 (www. vatican.va).

5. *The Cross and the Resurrection of Jesus*

He turned himself in for me: General audience, 27 November 2013 (www.vatican.va).

Learning how to embrace the cross: Homily on Palm Sunday, 24 March 2013 (www.vatican.va).

Together in pain and love: Speech at the Way of the Cross with young people, Copacabana, 26 July 2014 (www.vatican.va).

Before the sufferings of my Lord: Meeting with the priests at the Church of Gethsemane, 26 May 2014 (www.vatican.va).

From the slavery of sin to the freedom of love: *Urbi et Orbi* Message, 31 March 2013 (www.vatican.va).

Lent without Easter: *Evangelii gaudium*, 24 November 2013, nos. 6–8 (www.vatican.va).

In the joy of the Risen One: Regina Coeli, 21 April 2014 (www.vatican.va).

Walking towards the kingdom: General audience, 26 November 2014 (www.vatican.va).

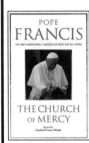
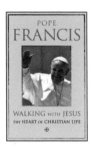
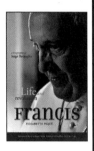